CREATIVITY
AND
IDENTITY
AN ARTIST'S SPIRITUAL QUEST

Creativity and Identity: An Artist's Spiritual Quest

Spiderwize
Remus House
Coltsfoot Drive
Woodston
Peterborough
PE2 9BF
www.spiderwize.com
A CIP catalogue record for this book is available from the British Library.
ISBN: 978-1-912694-27-3

CREATIVITY
AND
IDENTITY
AN ARTIST'S SPIRITUAL QUEST

SOPHIE ROSE PETERS

SPIDERWIZE
Peterborough UK
2018

Contents

I dedicate this book to:

- Giorgio Vasari for his book *The Lives of the Artists*

- The little artist in each of us who loves to create no matter what

- And finally, to all people who struggle with their sense of self: may your search bring you peace and love

INTRODUCTION

The book you hold in your hands is written subjectively from an artist's point of view. *Creativity and Identity: An Artist's Spiritual Quest* explores the inner landscape of one artist's striving towards a clear sense of self. This personal quest may be reflective of a general desire to be creative and to get in touch with our inner self.

Artists, therapists, parents of creative children and others interested in the artistic process will find much in the way of validation contained herein. Artists who are highly sensitive will especially benefit and know that they are in good company.

I explore not only what it means to be an artist but human growth and potential in general; touching on spirituality, religion and the desire for self-expression and inner peace. The hunger for beauty and light that is in us all is a golden thread that is weaved in gently throughout the book.

CHAPTER 1

TRUST – LET YOUR TRUE IDENTITY SHINE

I write this book from a position of enthusiasm and a desire to be of some help. I am an artist who also loves to swim. I love many things, but swimming is as natural for me as painting, though if we met socially I would say 'I am an artist' not 'I am a swimmer.' However, the two have many qualities in common. All the chapter titles can be applied to both practices, for that matter. I didn't always practice as an artist. In fact, for many years I felt lost. I wandered. I tried education and psychology, with very limited success as I didn't pursue them, although I love little children so learning about child education was very rewarding. Psychology is a hobby of mine. I especially enjoy reading about analytical psychology and I have found Jung and Jungian authors to be the most helpful to my creative spirit.

With this book I aim to share with you some of what I have experienced and learned and perhaps something from it will resonate with you. If you are feeling lost right now and frustrated – I deeply empathise. However, I would like to encourage you, in that if you take the time, effort and dedication to help yourself, you will make good headway. The search can be productive. If you are already doing what you love but are not yet financially successful, let me be honest, this is where I am at right now and I deeply trust that this can change for me and for you. So, in one way or another we have been in the same boat or are in the same boat. I feel successful in that I can do what I love, and it brings me happiness. Of course, to be able to share what I love and earn a living from it is truly the ideal. This ideal is, at present, an aim. So, what is your present aim?

Let me start by asking you directly: do you feel that you are an artist inside?

Artists are individuals who love beauty, order and harmony. In addition, genuine artists hate ugliness, disorder and chaos. They love life, colour, expression and freedom. It can take time to become a successful artist. Some have a knack for it whilst others need to learn some skills and other disciplines. This won't be a book on how to become financially successful, as I am not an expert in that. This might be a kind of mirror or guide as we find our way to our core selves. To the eternal self that doesn't change. The self that is timeless and magnificent no matter what our thoughts tell us about ourselves.

JOURNEY TO SELF

It may take some faith to journey to this self. Each day gives us a little light on the path. It may be helpful that others around us are on a similar search – some consciously, others less so. Perhaps a few not at all. You can usually tell from a brief conversation and the level of interest shown in this subject. In the privacy of reading and your own mind, you can make your own decisions. I trained as a life coach but as I have limited experience, this won't be a life-coaching book either. Think of me as a friend who has come to join you in your loneliness or in your solitude and is encouraging you to be your true self. The self who you love to be with when you are on your own and who perhaps only you know so well. If you are feeling lonely and frustrated with this search for your 'identity,' rest assured that you are among others searching too.

Let's consider Mother Nature for a while. If you take the time to just be *in nature* and observe her creatures, they are all doing their own unique 'thing.' They look and act like themselves. That's you and that's me. The way we look, the way we talk, what we say and how we feel inside all give clues as to who we are. We just need to pay attention. We need to listen to ourselves. We need to become aware and train ourselves to 'recognise ourselves.' How do we do this? Simply by observing. Have you ever noticed someone's behaviour that you found particularly pleasant? If you reflect, maybe you can give yourself some credit and notice that you are like this too. I would recommend focusing on the positives mostly. When we are lost we are a little afraid and can lean towards the negative. For the purpose of making searching for our identity enjoyable, I think it's nice and healthy to accentuate the positive. Once we are strong, we can look at the less appealing qualities. That doesn't mean we won't be aware of them – we just won't accentuate them.

Perhaps we've had enough of that in our early lives. If we've had a lot of criticism growing up, we can take up the habit and unconsciously re-enforce it. It's best to build up a gentle attitude with ourselves. There are plenty of people who are negative and intrusive out there so being good to ourselves gives us an advantage that will serve us well. When we don't do what we are naturally good at, and are gifted with, we struggle unnecessarily. It is painful because we are fighting our instincts to be creative. The strong urges that come through us to express ourselves are repressed and in turn we can become depressed. This is not constructive to our well-being and we need to take little steps away from depression towards expression. I write as a painter, so for me it is natural to work with brush, canvas and paint. When I do these things, I am happy. When I don't – for a long period of time – I become restless and irritable.

I recently read an article about an actress who suppressed her talent and didn't act. When she went to see a therapist, her therapist told her that she'd be unwell until she listens to her natural impulses and uses her talent. She did, and she regained her sense of well-being. Isn't it worth it? Aren't you worth it? Of course it is and of course you are! We all are. When we do what we are, we feel good. And feeling good is what is best for us. When we feel good we treat ourselves well and the reverse is also true. When we treat ourselves well, we feel good.

BEING TRUE TO OUR UNIQUENESS

So, when we are creative we are being true to our own uniqueness and expressing it. I know there may be some 'obstacles' but trust me on this; once you get busy doing what you love, the 'obstacles' will not seem as big. For instance, before you do your own painting you might look at the achievements of famous artists and feel overwhelmed. Once you do your work you are focused, and you begin to trust your own creation. And this trust can build into something beautiful inside you.

We can also be blocked by the negative stereotypes about artists. I won't write them down here because you are familiar with them. However, you are unique and you create your own path. Only you will define yourself in the process, and at the end of it all.

When I was doing my BA in Visual Communications I took a life drawing class as an option. Actually, I used to look longingly at the life drawing room and couldn't wait to sign up for that course. During that course, on one occasion a lovely model came up to me and said this: 'You're an artist.' I felt so happy inside that someone recognised me, but at that time I didn't quite allow that realisation to sink in. Of course I thanked her, but because on some deeper level I believed the negative stereotypes about artists, I didn't want to be one. At the same time, I read Irving Stone's biography on Michelangelo called *The Agony and the Ecstasy* and I was completely enthralled.

There was a longing and a pull the other way inside me at the time and it continued for a long time. Even though I was being creative on my course, I didn't see how I would make a living from doing it. This quest continues. I write because I love to write, and I so wish that there was a better infrastructure for helping artists make it and to be contributing members of society with their beautiful art. We exist to help make the world a more beautiful place to live and it would be amazing if society made this a little easier for us. I have found galleries reluctant to take on new artists, and all the rest we need to figure out somehow.

SEEKING VALIDATION

There are courses that would benefit artists for sure, on marketing, business and entrepreneurial thinking. I myself wish I had started to explore these less appealing but necessary courses while still at art school. We are creative people so 'money' doesn't tend to dominate our thoughts. Beauty does. But we still need to exist in a material world as well and buy our lovely tubes of paint, nice canvases and exciting brushes to work with!

We also need a lot of encouragement. Some more

so than others, but when this comes it is very good. When I got into a course on painting my tutor paid me a beautiful compliment when she said to me: 'You are such an artist Sophie.' Wow – I thought to myself – this sounds good. This rings true, especially since it was said with so much sincerity and it sounded very genuine. Unfortunately, not all my teachers were so very encouraging but that is also sadly part of life. There is good and there is bad. We need to extract the good and leave the bad behind. This can be a skill worthwhile learning in itself. Many artists are very sensitive people and negativity or criticism can be very hurtful and painful.

I wish I could offer a balm that would take all the pain away quickly, but we all learn individually how to deal with this. What I have learned is to consider the source and ask myself some questions. Do I like this person? Do I value this person's opinion? Is this person a good artist? And then consider my responses. I have also learned that the pain does pass and being creative regardless heals the wound. Of course, you have to clean the wound first! There is no need to pretend that it doesn't affect you or that you don't care.

SELF-CARE

Self-care is a must for artists. When people hurt us, we need to look after ourselves. We need to take some time to make sure that we protect ourselves and tend to our needs. Nurturing our **self** as well as our talent goes hand in hand. If this sounds like I am writing to a little child, well maybe there is something to it. Inside us is a vulnerable, creative soul, sensitive to the world around us. This is partly what makes us unique as artists. You might have noticed (perhaps with a little envy) that other people in other professions are not as highly sensitive as you. Even some artists you know are not as sensitive as you.

You are you and your soul matters, especially here. So, let's take care of it by being kind, gentle and wise. Other people who hurt you don't necessarily have to know the impact they have had on you, but you can tell people in your own way to back off if you feel it is justified. There are some people who have no sense of other people's boundaries and who are so out of touch with their own feelings that they are clueless about the effect that they have on others.

If we have suffered in our early lives, we may also need to re-learn to be patient with ourselves. I remember when I came back to my art and to painting after my years of wandering in the wilderness – as I call it – I not only felt a lot of fear and some self-doubt but I was also very impatient. I wanted to be good 'quickly.' I felt regret and remorse at what I then saw as my wasted years and wanted to make it all up 'now.' The one powerful consolation I did have was being creative. In fact, I loved every little stroke of the pencil, charcoal and paint that I was doing. All that mark-making felt liberating and exciting. I was having fun, even if my impatience was chasing me, mentally I felt happy.

The joy of seeing an image appearing on my paper or canvas filled me with a sense of hope and purpose that I simply never experienced working out the statistical results on my boring psychology course. As much as I loved being with little children, being a teacher held no interest for me. When I painted, however, I came alive. And this is what told me over and over again – despite my insecurities – that I am doing something really worthwhile and wonderful.

TWIST OF FATE

It was whilst I was working as an assistant teacher at a school teaching three and four year olds that a twist of fate happened. There I was, with my Montessori diploma all signed and sealed, working away at a little school. I loved the children and felt much joy being with them, but I hated teaching them how to write and do maths. They seemed so young and all they wanted to do was play, which I really understood. I wasn't enjoying my time there for other reasons too and I really wanted out.

Whilst working at the school I wasn't sure what I would do, but I had a dream. I dreamed I was doing something very colourful. I heard the words 'make-up artist' and that I would be successful. Well, not feeling confident I tried a weekend make-up artist course and knew for sure that wasn't it!

I signed up for a Saturday course at a local art school and for one day a week I came alive and enjoyed myself. When I asked the teacher where I could do a longer course he looked at me blankly. However, when someone I knew asked me about my art, the name of an art school literally floated into my mind like a soft white cloud. I knew that they offered a course in observational painting and I signed up. I had to create a portfolio and even though I had a feeling it wasn't all going to be a walk in the park, I was clear in my mind that I would do it. I did it and I have been painting steadily ever since.

My sense of self developed much slower than my art. I found the two and a half years at art school very tough going, and although I loved painting, I was very keen to finish and progress on my own for a number of reasons. I had a lot of practice at the school in observational work, and for that I am very grateful, but I didn't enjoy the rest. I love the freedom of doing my own thing!

On the course I had a teacher who complimented me on my painting of an orchid that I had included in a portrait. She said nothing about the figure but praised my flowers. Although at the time I felt offended that my figure seemed to be ignored, today I am very grateful for our brief conversation as that was all the encouragement I seemed to need to paint my subject matter which turned out to be flowers! So, it just goes to show that you never know where an experience or a conversation can take you. Trust your experiences and trust your life.

GETTING STARTED

Where does this leave you? Perhaps you see yourself in some aspects of my story, perhaps you don't, and you are still waiting for a revelation or a little enlightenment about how you can get started and have things fall into place for you. It will come. No person or book can say who you are for yourself. You get to define that for you, as we said earlier. But there may be some similarities that you recognise or that you identify with. Being an artist takes all sorts and even those of us who share this beautiful profession are different from one another. I may get excited about stunning flowers, but your passion might be horses or cars or scenery. Whatever it may be please don't give up until you find your special 'thing.'

It doesn't have to take a long time either. Once you make up your mind, things will start to happen and sooner or later, if you are paying attention, it will be right in front of you. It really does happen like that sometimes. You might be someone who loves to paint lots of different things. This is also good. Whatever floats your boat, as the saying goes. Just be tuned in and follow your heart. It will not lie to you and it will not let you down. You may need a bit of encouragement, but ultimately your heart is your best authority. Other people can guide you and help you, but you are the decision maker. If you feel shaky in yourself these may just sound like words at the moment, but as you get stronger you will see that this is true.

Our sense of self is built up, I believe, from how we

treat ourselves over the course of the day. When we are good and kind to our 'self' we have a 'good day.' When we are harsh with ourselves we have a 'bad day.' It may seem like someone else has affected us for better or worse and this is the reason why we feel good or bad, and perhaps this has a role to play. Still, as we become aware of our responses and reactions, we can modify things to moderate our internal 'temperature.'

SELF-REGULATION

This way we become much better able to self-regulate and we won't be so much at the mercy of others. Just try it and see if this rings true for you. Next time someone says something negative, leave it for a while before you respond and you might feel a sense of inner control building up within you. From this position you become much more powerful in your own life than if you had simply retaliated. You might even let this person leave your life. Isn't that a good thing? You want kind people in your life!

So, this chapter introduced trust. As we respond to our inner promptings and start to follow our heart we become more in touch with our inner self and our talents. We begin to pursue what we love, and circumstances often come to our aid to help us take the next step and the next on our own path. As we look back we can see the invisible guiding hand shaping our lives. Through good times and bad we listen to that still small voice within and begin our journey with trust. We then begin to get a glimpse of joy.

CHAPTER 2

JOY – THE SUNSHINE IN YOUR SOUL

Art is something that comes from the heart. The shape of our heart and the feelings contained therein are unique to each of us. None is fashioned alike. Each heart must sing her own song and paint her own pictures. What my heart loves may be very different to what your heart loves and this is what makes our hearts special and worth listening to. They are talking to us all the time. When we look at a work of art we know in our hearts whether it moves us or not, regardless of its fame or market value.

When I worked with little children and watched their joy as they coloured, it was clear as daylight that they were putting their hearts into their work. Their feelings were expressed in the colours they were choosing and using. Often, they would be talking or singing to themselves as they worked. They were filled with joy. They were loving what they were doing. This comes through in the work of children and it comes through in the work of enthused adults.

We love the passion of Van Gogh and we delight in the free spirited and fun elements of Matisse's work.

To be colouring is to be having fun. We can tune into the world of colour. Inside the classroom observing little children, outside in nature or in an art gallery. The colours that artists use are their guiding light in creating beautiful paintings that capture minds and hearts and move souls. Colours inspire when they are in harmony. When there is no harmony, the discord it generates is unpleasant and the work is not very valuable to the human spirit, which relies on comforting and nourishing sustenance.

COLOUR

This nourishing quality of colour is of vital importance. A healthy life is infused with colour. In my opinion, a person who loves colour is a healthy person who loves life. There is no life without colour. We seek it in the food we eat, in the clothes we wear, and we appreciate its vibrancy in nature. Anyone who is feeling sad benefits from the beautiful effects of colour in a well-painted picture. It is little wonder that the Impressionists are so universally popular.

Again, when we watch the unique colouring technique of children, we see that the way they work with colour is really beyond technique. It is pure intuition. The pinks go with the reds and the oranges go with the greens and so on – they pick their colours as they 'feel' them. This is the glory and mystery of colour application. To feel and do. Not to study every technique under the sun and then to produce dead looking art.

Of course, knowledge of colour theory is of immense value. It is worth studying and practising. But then it is advisable to just feel one's way and play. And to always to be observing and learning from nature, children and other artists whose colour work you admire. I include children because the ones among them who enjoy colouring are really natural at it. They feel so free when they colour. I suspect it is because they are feeling at one with the process and their enjoyment flows from the heart.

GROWTH

As we are talking about identity as well as creativity, let's be clear that the human being is developing continuously at all stages and ages. Because of this development, growth needs to be tended to attentively and sensitively. How one goes about working on his inner being is a skill that can be learned at an early age from home, if that home life was loving, nurturing and supportive. If these elements were missing, one need not despair but should go in search of anything that supports her growth now, be it from a therapist or other loving and good people.

Of course, one needs, in this case, to become especially responsive to one's own needs and heed them. Not all lives have been given an equal or positive start, but that can be slowly and steadily rectified with some help. It is good to ask for positive support. To heal oneself and to bring together all the disparate elements of one's identity, a creative person requires a suitable and qualified person. There is no need to suffer in silence when help exists and can be actively sought.

As an artist works with colour she will find that colour has many healing properties. It is a joy to see the radiance of colours playing in harmony on a canvas that is the product of one's creative efforts. It stills the mind and invites love towards one's work. This is all very beneficial. As we love our work we may yet begin to see that we can love ourselves. We can create! We can bring forth beautiful images. This is good news. We are contributing to something positive by being creative. We are not sitting idle watching the world go by and wandering why more good things are not happening to us, but instead we are rejoicing in the fruit of our hands and the love of our creative hearts.

BEING ARTISTIC

Now we are artists and we are being artistic. Actually, I think an artist is always being artistic. We see something ugly and it bothers our senses and so we seek out beauty. We admire the beauty around us and we can appreciate its presence. These simple artistic 'habits' are the mark of an artistic soul.

Whenever someone asks me why I am an artist I

reply, 'I am in it for the colour.' Colour is my passion. I love it. I think of it so highly that I order my world around it. I like to live in a colourful home and I like to wear colourful clothes. I feel better for it. I live simply – my favourite outfit is a pair of jeans with a colourful top – but still I opt for colour. I love to have flowers in my home to brighten up the scenery and they cheer me up very easily.

When I was a little girl living in Budapest, Hungary (which is where I am originally from) I remember that whenever I had the chance to draw something I would typically draw a parrot (for its colours) and a palm tree. This tropical pairing enchanted me and stirred my imagination. I was always happy with this image. Perhaps it has a message for me today – I don't know. Maybe I'll think of it or discover it. For me, the parrot's colours truly sing of a strong identity. Would you agree? Colour gives nature's creatures a distinction that is very strong. Whether it is a flower or a butterfly, the colours signal something original.

When in search for our identity, I believe we are also looking for what makes us an 'original.' I think an artist is already unique in society, whether a particular society appreciates that artist or not, because she is fulfilling her role of being an artist. Just by being what one is supposed to be there is a greater sense of joy and peace. Of course, we can interrupt that joy and peace by questioning ourselves, our roles, our identity and our 'market value', but this is, in my experience, fruitless.

HEALTHY SELF-IMAGE

It is far better and more constructive to work on developing a positive and healthy self-image, one based on the truth of who we are rather than being aggressive towards ourselves. This aggression can be a result of comparing ourselves to others (unfavourably) or putting ourselves down for not 'fitting in.'

We need to 'fit in' with ourselves. As we value ourselves and our work, we begin to feel more at home in our bodies. This may take some time and practice but it's worth it. Artists are sometimes sidelined in a society that is more materialistically minded because, well, how is art necessary or practical? I find it necessary because it matters to the artist to create and it is practical because painting is actually very grounding. I know when I paint I am completely present and focused.

This helps me to be more present and focused when I am spending time with someone and I can listen to that person. The question of money and economic value is something that an artist needs to work out for themselves. However, money does not equal a person's worth. Of course, having one's work sell is a mark of appreciation and that is of immense value, not just to an artist but to anyone. We love to be appreciated!

STUDY AND SEEKING RELEVANCE

When I was at art school studying painting I really enjoyed reading autobiographies or books on artists I admired. I considered it a part of my training. Their problems seemed to reflect some of mine and I often found consolation in my struggles reading about theirs. It helped me with my thoughts of *it is only I who has ever felt like this* and expanded my awareness that others have gone through the same thing. The lack of recognition of many of their stories made me feel at once sober and sad. Sober because it reflects some reality and sad because artists need to earn a living from their work and deserve money for their labour of love, like anyone else. Not all artists (myself included) are happy self-promoters. We prefer the quiet option and meeting with people on a personal basis.

I recently had someone tell me that 'modesty doesn't sell.' I didn't say anything at the time. In my thoughts I simply said, 'I'll keep that in mind,' secretly wondering about this person. I personally like to buy from a person who is not shouting about their work but simply and honestly presenting it for people to benefit from and enjoy. But we are all different. Some artists are quieter about it, preferring their work to speak for itself, whilst others love to be loud about it. It takes all sorts. I would just stick with what feels natural and comfortable for you. If you are on the quiet end it may take longer, but you will have stayed true to yourself and that is always better than going against your nature and doing something you detest.

An artist loves to draw and colour. Drawing and designing is the very foundation of being an artist. It is how we describe what we see. I prefer to draw things from life. For this reason, I was very happy to be involved with life drawing as a fundamental step in me becoming a painter and to this day I like to draw something I see in front of me. For a year and a half, I went every week to the National Gallery in London to draw from the paintings. It was never something I loved as I would often feel a little self-conscious, but I loved the results and I especially appreciated the kindness of the public.

I was often surprised how they were so much more encouraging than many of the people, including some of the teachers, whom I met at art school. At art school it is so easy to think that on some level the teachers know it all and that is why they are teaching, but really as one steps away from that often strange world and into the often healthier environment of the broader world, nice surprises await! So, if you are at art school and there is a lack of encouragement I would encourage you to try public places for some vital oxygen.

FINDING JOY

We all benefit from people saying nice things about our work. It just feels positive and praise is good. When I was doing my BA, I went on a two-week work experience to an advertising agency, imagining at that time that I wanted to be a copywriter. I was soon disillusioned. One lunchtime I happened to walk into a bookstore and came across what was then a bright blue book with a colourful handprint on it. The title? '*The Artist's Way*' by Julia Cameron.

I bought it, filled with excitement, and read it with much gladness in my heart. Here was an author who spoke to me and understood what I wanted to do. I really like that book, and if you are in need of a knowledgeable and friendly guide for starting on your journey, I recommend Julia's book.

The matter of joy in being an artist is crucial. Joy of the work will carry you through the peaceful times as well as the more turbulent times. I remember that especially in the early days of going to my studio, soon after I finished the course, it was really the joy of doing the work that kept me going. This feeling anchored me when I was beset with doubts about what I am doing and where painting my flowers will take me. I wanted a crystal ball that would tell me that everything was going to be alright, that there is a beautiful hidden purpose to all this training and hard work and that it will pay off. I think I wanted success to be, well, a little easier!

I wanted to show myself and 'the world' that I am capable of standing on my own two feet and making a living doing what I love, since that is what I wanted most of all. I had suffered through the years of wilderness, of wandering, of 'not knowing' who I am and what on Earth I was supposed to be doing. I took on boring jobs that were joyless and jobs that didn't feel personally rewarding to me. I studied psychology – a subject that I loved reading about – but discovered to my dismay that as an academic subject it felt dead to me. A Montessori qualification led me into the world of children and child development, as well as observing children doing art and playing.

Later, figurative painting, as a study as well as a form of play, for me had multiple rewards. Not only is it good for developing skills in drawing from life, if one is a sensitive person that sensitivity will feed into the painting and the result will be more life-like. It can also help develop one's empathy for the person who is modelling. I once read in a Christian women's magazine about a life model who saw her work as her special calling and destiny to help artists in developing their skill and talent. I felt deep respect and admiration for her. She also knew who she was and why she was doing her profession.

PAINTING

Painting people helps enormously with one's power of observation when it comes to the human face and what a face can reveal about the underlying personality. Of course, this all takes time, patience and skill. Painting is not there to judge people but rather to discern the varieties of characters who surround us. It is also a lot of fun to learn to paint from live human beings and at the time I did it I enjoyed it very much.

So, whatever way you chose to develop your art and to hone your skills, it is best done with enjoyment. It need not feel like drudgery. If it feels like you are dragging your heels through a course of study or a way of life it might be time to check in with yourself and ask yourself some honest questions. And then listen to the answers that you get back from yourself! If art remains at the centre of your heart, please persist, either with the course if you are benefitting in some way, or find a way to learn that best suits you.

If you are an artist let the wonder of colour infuse your work, fire your imagination, and let it bring you a sense of this precious joy we have been talking about. It is good to feel happy as we work. Colour is king, the artist is his queen. They go together and have done throughout the ages.

The joy of colouring can be transmitted through the experience of tending to our inner nature and shaping our identity as we go along. We all know how

Michelangelo said that really, he was just releasing the existing form from the marble with his sculpting. We need to be as sensitive to our own form and chip away with skill. Our best self is in there waiting to be discovered and released.

CHAPTER 3

PROCESS – DISCOVERING OUR PURPOSE

Ah! The hope of finding a purpose in life. I think this needs to be approached in a friendly and relaxed way. Of course, when we are still unsure of who we are and what it is we are going to create, both with our paintings and with our lives, we have a tendency to feel restless and impatient. This is natural. It can be very frustrating trying different careers and feeling unsettled. Sooner or later an artist needs to accept that she is not something else or someone else, but she is an artist and she is herself with strengths and weaknesses like other human beings.

This might sound very obvious, but my experience has been that when we feel unsure of our identity as artists, we long to be something other. We look at what other people are doing and if things are going well for them, and if they are successful we might wonder whether we should be doing what they are doing.

I think also that as artists because we are creative and we love to learn, it is especially easy and seductive to think that we are suited to and adaptable to other professions. This is not necessarily so. We might not always love the isolation of the work, even though we know deep inside that we love and we need solitude. Some artists prefer to work with others and they arrange their working life to reflect this. However, many prefer to work on their own in the privacy of their homes or studios with their own choice of subject matter and surroundings.

There is both a price and a pay-off to working as an artist. The price is that the rewards we seek and would like to have might take time to create or to come our way. Recognition may or may not come to us. Money may or may not come quickly or easily. We may need to develop skills that seem foreign to us and we may not, at first, feel comfortable with. The pay-off is doing what we love. So, we balance these and other things in our minds and we make a decision.

FIRST THINGS FIRST

These are all part of the process. First, we need to learn and develop our craft. Without some basic training, we are not much different to people who do not put in time to become competent at what they do. It may be frustrating to start with, baby steps, but I think looking at the development of a human being is a good analogy to becoming a fully-fledged artist. First there is conception. We recognise and admit to ourselves that we are artists. Then we develop in the womb of some kind of container, usually a creative course of some kind. Then we are released from this womb or classroom into the world. We may at first have someone help us out and we learn to crawl, walk, run – in our own way and at our own pace – until we can take care of all of the areas of being an artist. This may or may not reflect your ideas or experience, but this has been my path.

I have personally found that I can only focus on one thing at a time otherwise I feel overwhelmed. At art school I focused on developing my art skills and then my next step was fulfilling my other dream, which was doing a life-coaching training course since I had always wanted to be of help to other people who are creative and wanted to fulfill their dreams.

Writing this book is my way to being of help in however small a way, as I want to commit now to being successful as an artist. This is what matters the most to me as I think we are all at our most inspiring when we make 'our own thing' work and become successful, both as people and as artists.

Engaging with other people who can help us is very useful. I thought that I could do everything on my own, but it turns out that I was wrong. I think I felt embarrassed to admit that I needed help. Fortunately, (at least in London, and I suspect this is true elsewhere and hopefully in your area) there are many opportunities and platforms for new learning.

There are books which are easy to access and there are several adult learning institutions or lectures given, often for a small sum, in major and local libraries. We are also lucky to have some events given for free. This is all worthwhile to look into and make the most of, as you never know where they can lead to and you might meet some really good people.

OPPORTUNITIES

It might at first seem daunting, if you are used to working on your own a lot, to suddenly go to events like these, but it does get easier and in time you will have wondered, as I did, why you didn't do it sooner. For me, the truth is it didn't even occur to me until someone pointed it out. Sometimes the obvious needs to be said! Even things we read in books or some other form of print don't come to life until we have a conversation with someone about something that matters to us.

Our purpose is something that we discover or uncover or come into alignment with as we do our work. This is why I suggested at the beginning of the chapter to take a light hearted approach to it. I know we all want to feel useful and connected, and hopefully be recognised for our efforts and contributions, but even getting to this stage takes time and work. The yearning for recognition is natural but we need to have the work ready in order to be recognised. The nice thing is that as this is all a process, even early on our journey we can start to get the little recognitions that can mean so much to us.

When the lovely life model told me that I am an artist in my BA life drawing class that mattered to me and

I will never forget her. She became a very important person in my life and she just came over to me and said it in a very natural and casual way. It is the same when my tutor at art school praised my work and was encouraging to me. Luckily, I got on with her and she was one of the reasons, as well as pursuing my painting, that I stuck out that particular course.

And if you think about it and reflect on your own life for a moment, you will see that you have met such good people as well. When you are getting any kind of praise or encouragement from someone or somewhere you are on the right path. It may not seem obvious, but you are also *on purpose*. This is especially true if somewhere in the depths of your heart and in your private moments you know that you are doing the right thing, even though the path seems difficult and not clearly planned out for you.

NO CLEAR PATH

As artists this is especially true since there is no clear career path. We can go to classes and do courses but after that it is up to us to create our own path. This is both scary and exciting. I think the best thing to do is to tell ourselves that we can do it and to trust that everything that we need to know will come to us at the right time. If we miss something, it will come. Patience and energy to make things happen are important though.

We need patience to persevere and we need the

energy to make things happen that will benefit us. I imagine that I am reminding you of things that you already know, but reminders can be good. Swimming relaxes me as well as giving me positive energy. It might be running or dancing or yoga for you! Whatever gives you this buzz, it is worth appreciating and doing it regularly. As artists and human beings, we need to take care of our health: mental, emotional, physical and spiritual. We also need to give ourselves time off to rest and yes, even to day dream a little!

We can learn from the lives of other artists (such as the ones Vasari wrote about) or others whom we admire. There is no point in burning out. We can do things at our own pace. We are not in competition with each other or with anyone else. If you are, I recommend asking yourself why. Trust that you and your work are unique, original and one of a kind. There is no need to hurry or to worry. There is simply a need to do your work, to be happy and to be a decent human being.

A DIM LIGHT

As we do our work and grow as artists, we might catch a glimpse of our purpose on the horizon. It may be a dim light at first, that begins to rise and appears to come towards us. Our job is to get in our boat and meet this rising purpose with a sense of adventure and optimism. What might your purpose be saying to you now? A clue is that it is not coming from the great beyond, but as something quiet from within yourself.

Having trained as an artist and as a life coach, I really want to play a role in helping all of us be successful at what we do. We train to be artists and put our love into our work for it to be valued and appreciated. Naturally, we cannot guarantee that everyone will value our work the way that we do, but we are trusting that what we like doing would have appeal to other human beings in the world who want to live with what we create.

It is also a worthwhile pursuit to inspire other people. Whether we are artists, therapists, coaches, parents, teachers or friends, we want the people who we come into contact with to feel good about themselves and to reach for their best. So, it follows from this that we want to do our best. When we don't try, we are left with negative and uncomfortable feelings of letting ourselves down. By comparison, when we do our best we feel good, energised, positive and happy to take new chances and to grow. Stagnation feels frustrating and boring whereas growth feels enlivening, dynamic and progressive.

Self-reliance is a good thing and so is reaching out and asking for help. For artists who are highly sensitive sometimes the outside world can feel overwhelming and threatening. Elaine Aron's book *The Highly Sensitive Person* goes into excellent detail about having this trait and if you feel so inclined, it is a very good as well as practical read.

GETTING TO KNOW ONESELF

Working with a skilful therapist can also help take the edge of some of those powerful feelings that irritate our sensitivity and discharge unhelpful emotions. Getting to know oneself deeply and intimately is also the best road to feeling more comfortable with oneself, as well as other people whom we choose to have close to us. Elaine Aron is an excellent guide for highly sensitive people in this. There is no substitute for a good therapist if you need one. You may find other resources to help you deal with the many things that are going on inside of you.

Honesty is your best friend. Being honest with yourself about your strengths and limitations, as and when they crop up in your daily life, will not let you down. Developing and trusting one's intuition and instincts, not just about the use of colour on the canvas, but about the people you meet and the opportunities that come your way, is a must. Learn about these skills and practice. Some people think artist are 'naïve' or 'too trusting' or 'too sensitive' and so on. If you've had these labels or have come across people who have talked about you in this way, you will know what I am talking about. I consider being sensitive 'normal' for many artists.

I say this because we are living in a feeling and natural world. It is unnatural to be completely insensitive. Having said this, we can suffer from the negative reactions of our sensitivities. Just being mindful of this, we can ease off ourselves and learn to make less of a big deal about our reactions or responses to things, people or events. Even if things don't work out for us and we make a fuss, it will pass. It always does. Patience with ourselves will help a lot.

PASSION AND VIRTUE

The best way to make it in anything (as long as one likes and enjoys it, as well as having skills in it) is to keep doing it. There is no magic formula, no genie in a bottle that grants us our wish of bliss and eternal success. Just doing it is what gives meaning to our days, weeks and years. It is the fuel that keeps the engine running. It is the passion that recharges and flows from our heart. It is how we grow from little seedlings into flowers. This is how we attract the good that is wanting to come into our lives.

When we have something to offer we naturally signal that we are ready. This is not to say that we are nothing and nobody until we have created enough work to fill a palace. That would simply not be true, and it would be dismissive of our human value. However, all of us need to develop virtue and character. The most important virtue is love. We are all attracted to people who are loving and kind. They are beautiful. They shine. We want to be like them. We may already be like them, but we still need to develop these qualities in ourselves or simply to shine a light on them.

Think for a moment of the most loving person you

know. How do you feel around or with this person? I imagine you get nice, warm feelings and you feel good. This is love. It attracts, and it makes those who come into its aura feel good. Hopefully our art has the same effect! For me, beauty is very closely linked to love. Whatever is beautiful is lovable and whatever is lovable is beautiful. It doesn't have to be perfect to be lovable or beautiful. This is not the same thing. But it does have to be special. Just like we cannot love everybody, not everybody loves us. As long as we know inside that we are lovable, and even likeable, that is what matters. So often if we are struggling with our identity, we are also struggling with our sense of being lovable. This is sad, but it can be changed. We need not struggle all our lives.

LOVE AND FORGIVENESS

Many, many people have struggled and have won. You can too, and I can too. Good teachers have all taught about the value of forgiveness. I will not talk much about it here – I am just mentioning it. An excellent book that explores this subject is Simon Wiesenthal's book *The Sunflower*. I think we all come to forgiveness in our own way in our own time. When I once discussed this subject with someone, that person observed in our conversation that forgiveness comes from the heart.

Maybe our real purpose in life is to love. This can manifest in all kinds of ways and your way is unique to you, as my way is unique to me. Maybe you are destined to love a certain group of people whom you can help, in a way that is completely special to you and no one can do it like you. Or maybe you are destined to love just one person completely. It can transpire in unknown ways and the invitation will be there when we are ready for it.

Perhaps you are feeling very lonely in your life right now and you are wondering if things will ever change for you. It might be that you are feeling stuck and want very much for a sign to show you the way or some charming person to rescue you. It is alright to fantasise and day dream, and then find a way to support yourself and your feelings. Being lonely can be painful and difficult. But in my experience the best solution to feeling lonely is to find a way to connect with your thoughts and feelings and find out what is going on inside of you, so that you don't feel so alienated from yourself. It might be that you are in pain about something and you have not connected with that pain but rather you are suppressing it and pushing it down.

BEING HUMAN

Pain is not pleasant, but it is especially more difficult if it is not acknowledged and felt. And then it needs to be released. Whether that involves praying about it, writing it down, or talking it through with someone who you trust. Ignoring pain is like ignoring a two-year-old who is having a tantrum or a little child who is crying. If you go down to their level, show empathy for their feelings and comfort them, then that child will slowly relax and eventually will feel better. It is the same with your pain.

So being an artist and developing as a human being go in tandem. There have been artists we have all heard of who developed their work but let themselves go. This is not ideal. We are people first and then we are artists. Learning to take care of ourselves needs to be our top priority. I am sure that you know this. Becoming who we are is a process and our purpose reveals itself as we go along, when we are ready for it. There is no rush and it is best to leave aside competing.

We need only to appreciate our own work and be with others who reflect this back to us. Our identity comes with a sense of 'I' and 'I am.' And then list all the good things like 'I create beautiful art,' and 'I am a talented artist.' Making strong positive statements to ourselves about ourselves helps us be the loving people we are created to be.

CHAPTER 4

SKILL – LEARNING TO SEE AND FEEL WITH THE HEART

Our eyes are beautiful, sensitive organs that register the world to our minds, bodies and souls. For those of us lucky enough to have the faculty of our eyes, it is a gift to see and to tune into beauty. An artist does this wholeheartedly when she trains her eyes to consider what is truly lovely to behold. What is lovely to me has the qualities that resonate within our hearts as we look at them.

Beauty is often very simple and very natural. We have the whole of the natural world to wonder at and we have our inner sense of 'knowing' about what feels good to us to look at. We have the masterpieces of artists long gone but whose work fills the galleries of the world. When we walk through a gallery, very often a painting will speak to us. It will either convey a mood or a message or simply its excellence. Beauty is excellence made manifest.

The greatest artists make art look easy and effortless. We know from reading about their lives and from our own experience that excellence takes practice and skill.

When we have the skill for something and we practice with diligence and dedication, we get better at it. And we can keep improving to our heart's content.

As an artist it is essential that we love our profession. It can be a struggle at times because it can seem so precarious financially. But it is best to exercise faith and, when doubt comes, to thank our great God for creating us to be artists. I have found this simple practice most practical and helpful. Rather than lament about my difficulties as I give thanks, I tune into the goodness of being an artist and being in the wonderful position to be doing what I love: creating beautiful paintings.

Art does carry with it the quality to inspire enthusiasm of the dedicated artist. Painting is actually very enjoyable. It is so because it is both a challenge and a great joy. Together, these generate a feeling of wanting to keep going and doing what we love most. When we are happy with our chosen subject matter we feel a natural reverence. I find that this extends beyond painting flowers for me, for example, into feeling a reverence for all things beautiful and fragile. We talked about this being a feeling universe. Every creature under the sun, including nature, is responsive to light, to sound, to touch and to energy in general.

As artists, part of our identity includes being identified with what is wholesome, what is good and what is natural. There is no benefit, to my mind, in generating or identifying with what is ugly or immoral. We can best shape our identity and character by being tuned in to what our profession calls us: conveyors of beauty. We bring to life on the canvas what is in our hearts as we respond to the subject we have chosen to paint. This bringing to life, this act of creation, is what sparks the joy and sense of aliveness that makes art and painting so worthwhile.

LEARNING AND DEVELOPING

We learn and develop as we go along. We may want to be under a 'master' or we may decide after a period of study to go it alone and be more independent in our creative expression. If one is sensitive to the comments of others, in my experience it is a good idea to go it alone for a while and develop our own unique painting voice. As artists we are original and originators. We can learn a lot from other people, and we learn the most from the great masters of ages past, and by doing what we are born to do.

Mastery takes time. But all along we are picking up ideas and letting other ideas go. We are shaping our art and we are forging our own path. It gets to be a colourful adventure as we beaver away in our studios. But there are issues as well. Whilst it can be freeing to be solitary in our studios, in my experience existential questions arise outside of it. Who am I? What am I doing? Why am I doing it? Where am I going with all this? Who will buy my art? And so on with all such 'W' questions.

I have a lovely card painted by Renee Locks with the

words: 'A bird does not sing because it has an answer. It sings because it has a song.' Maybe we can settle these questions for now with this simple attitude. We each have a song and our hearts want to sing it with colours on a canvas. So, we just do it and leave the existential questions for a time when we they are ready to reveal themselves to us.

Without some level of ingenuity, it is difficult to pass off as an original artist. We need to have some kind of vision; something to aim for and something to work towards. We need, above all, to feel inspired and to be led from within. There is a whole world out there questioning the existence of art and artists, so we need massive courage and resilience to keep doing what we are good at. Luckily, there are also many good people who love and value art and feel inspired by original art.

INSPIRATION

Inspiration is a beautiful gift that we can give with our art. It's wonderful when people look at the art or buy it because it connected with them and communicated with their own inner being. If you've sparked off a fire of passion in a would-be artist – even better!

I imagine that there are many artists who value the work of other artists and want to connect with them and share their vision and their thoughts. As a student I would often write to artists whose work I admired or touched me in some way and it was always a source of joy and pleasure when they would respond with something encouraging. We are meant to help one another to the best of our ability. Of course, we are just one person and we may not always have the time, the resources or energy, but we can all do something. Children especially need our love and encouragement when they are being creative, because that is when they are most themselves and also most vulnerable. They too, love being appreciated for their cheerful sunshine, flowers, houses and butterfly pictures!

Sometimes good things happen by chance. My vision opened up before me as I read a small book on Cezanne. In the whole book there was a tiny image of a Matisse painting, which was of a simple still life against a patterned background. My 'seeing and feeling eyes' popped wide open and I instantly perceived that this is what I could do with my flowers. And this is how I started my flower art in my studio. I painted flowers against beautifully patterned backgrounds. So, my suggestion to you, if you are struggling with a 'vision', is to trust your 'intuition' and stay tuned to the magical and whimsical nature of Lady Chance who will happily grace your life if you stay open to her.

NO SHORT CUTS

There really are no short cuts in life to anything that we truly desire. In my short life experience, this has been true, certainly with 'love' and definitely with 'success'. I have come to accept that practice is the only way to develop my skill, and patience and preparation are part of the road to success. We all want to be successful and it is confounding when this is not happening 'now'. But 'now' is very real and very much happening. We have power in the now to create and live the life we want to live. We can act in the now and plan for the future.

I think that in our minds time is very flexible and fluid. Sometimes we are in the 'past' state and at other times we are in the 'present' or 'future' state. So how can we use this awareness to our advantage?

As human beings we have problems that we need to solve. Many authors write books to help people with 'how to' solve their problems. We can turn to these authors and other helpful people for guidance and we can also develop trust in ourselves to become skillful at solving problems. We can use art and painting as a strong metaphor for solving problems and apply these lessons to the practical problems that we face. Maybe we can even do this for the emotional issues that we have inside us wanting to be resolved. When we paint we need to prepare. I had a teacher once who said that preparation is fifty per cent of the work done. I have always liked this. I felt good thinking that once I had everything I needed in front of me I was half-way through my 'work.'

So, going back to our approach to problem solving we take the first step, which is preparation. We gather resources to help us get clarity. And then we use our tools to begin our work. These tools are paintbrushes for our paintings, but they may be a simple pad and pen for the 'problem' that we are facing. We need to be clear what the problem is. Once we have done this we shut out distractions and we focus on the work at hand. So, in painting we squeeze out the colours that we need, we draw the image and then we colour it in. In the real world, focusing on the problem rarely works. We need to tune into the beautiful world of solutions. They are out there, and they are also inside us. To my mind, a solution is often very simple, often 'obvious' and often difficult to track down! So, what do we do?

FINDING SOLUTIONS

We develop our skill in finding solutions just like we develop our painting. For example, at art school we are working on developing our drawing and painting skills. Many of us are not being taught how to market our work, how to price our work and how to find enthusiastic customers. But in the real world we need to be able to find a solution to the problem of selling our artwork. For the quiet and reticent among us, this can seem very off-putting.

Luckily, there are many wonderful resources and people who can help us and we can connect with the ones that align with our values and our vision. For those of us who prefer to be pleasant and not loud with our marketing, there are marketing and entrepreneurial books that use a gentler tone. In this we do have a say and a degree of control. Just like in painting, we choose the 'materials' and the resources that are best suited to our nature, our personality and our work.

If you are terrified and feel 'clueless' about how to 'sell' – take heart. There are books and people who can help. It just takes a bit of grit and persistence to connect with the right resources. Also, one has to put aside the fear of not knowing about 'business' and having funny ideas about 'money.' We all need money and developing a good attitude – that is one of curiosity and respect – towards it helps. For artists, this energy of money is a friendly resource enabling us to continue with our work; buying our colours and creating more pictures to sell. You may also consider other avenues if business is not your strength.

I wonder: how do you feel about the two little words 'to sell?' For an artist to sell their work is incredibly exciting, liberating and energising. We can feel amazing that someone has so appreciated our work that they want to take it home and live with it! After all, isn't this why we do it? Of course, painting makes us happy, but when someone wants it – it really is the icing on the cake. We have made something that communicates the love we have put into it to another human being. Wonderful! So, the two little words 'to sell' really mean that we have 'done well!'

DOING WELL

And we all want to do well! Naturally we are doing well anyway, but this is an addition to all the joy and fun we have been having painting away. We have 'sold!' This can be a nice little feather in our cap and give us a little bounce as we walk down the street and widen our smile. The world is better because of a happy artist. Our hearts are happy and trust me, a happy heart creates happy art. Matisse once remarked that he wished to stay away from depressing subject matter and make pictures that make other people happy. I find this very healthy.

This is my personal philosophy as well. There is enough sadness and there is enough pain in our lives, so when we take the time to paint it is liberating to create paintings that are actually full of joy and radiating love. Love is very powerful and our love for our work will not let us down. Love will find a way for us to be successful. Don't fret or feel bad if you are not a marketing wizard. Neither am I and neither are a lot of artists. Just try your best to find a way to have your art be seen. It is, of course, a decision to step out of our cosy studios and face the world. This happens inside us and it is a pro-active decision.

Perhaps you have already taken some steps. Even

if you feel a bit hesitant and very new to all this 'information', I encourage you to persist. Do you remember how you first felt when you started to paint? Or your first visit to an art shop? Well, that was new too, and you learned, and you coped, and you got more confident. It is the same with business. Anything can be learned, especially when we have a desire, a motivation or a situation of necessity.

I like to think that as I have been put on this Earth to paint and make people happy with my art, there are people on this Earth who want to see my art and buy it. I love buying things that enhance my life and I am sure that in this respect there are others who feel the same.

Owning a work of art that is personally meaningful is very special. I know this because I made a small purchase from a French artist who was showing in London. It's a very small painting of a woman in a flowing white dress holding a bouquet of colourful flowers. I knew I wanted it as soon as I saw it because I thought to myself 'this is me!' And that was it. I bought it and I met another lovely artist, which was an additional bonus for me.

An artist is resourceful. We can remember this quality in ourselves as we embark on our vocation, once we are on it and as we broaden our horizons. We can make use of our signature strengths to become more successful in bringing our art to an audience who would appreciate it and value the people who love our art. Developing skill and mastery in our craft comes first I believe. We need to offer something that is good and that we feel good about offering. We can meet our challenges with the same attitude that we bring to our work: dedication, clarity, focus, honesty and experimenting with ideas.

No two artists create paintings that are alike, so we can value our uniqueness. In a similar vein, no two people go about selling their work in the same way, so it is worthwhile to keep an open mind and to witness how we prefer to do this. Being true to ourselves, to our work and to our values will bring their own fruit. Learning to make a living from our art is a skill that we can build for our benefit and for the benefit of others. As we develop this skill we can grow in our confidence as artists who are willing to be of service to our fellow human beings by bringing the joy and beauty.

CHAPTER 5

PRACTICE – CREATING COURAGEOUSLY

Those artists who practice their art separate themselves from those who do not. Practice, for those who do it, becomes a form of dedication to their work and it allows for inspiration to flow naturally. It takes less effort to practice continuously and follow one's natural inclination, than to sit idly by and hope for the creative muse to appear. This is not to say that one has to be always beavering away with no time for rest and recreation, but it's just best to keep doing one's work quietly and trusting that this self-application to one's work will yield good results. The results are in the work. It is very satisfying for an artist to see her skills developing. For me, each time I sit down to do my painting feels, in a way, like the first time. No two pictures are the same. Even though my subject matter is flowers, I aim to create a new image every time I paint. This keeps my work fresh and my ideas interesting to me.

I have known people, as I am sure we all have, who are very talented but are, for some reason, reluctant to show up and do their work. This is a pity because where talent is a gift, one's involvement in developing it is up to the individual. Of course, life is generous and provides many opportunities for the lapsed artist to come back and re-apply herself. It's happened in my life. Grief, sorrow, loss or other difficult life experiences can deplete the heart and there may need to be a time to turn inwards and to heal. But my experience is that creativity is a great healer.

Even if one doesn't feel like doing anything creative, a mark on a paper can be very encouraging for the soul. A Jungian analyst, Marie Louise von Franz, is quoted in the book *Carl Jung and Soul Psychology* as saying this: 'Nothing in the human psyche is more destructive than unrealised, unconscious creative impulses.' I think this a sobering statement from someone with a lot of experience helping people recover their sense of self.

BEING CREATIVE

An artist is creative in her DNA, so the need to be creative is as strong in her as the need to breathe. It is sad that there are many voices in an artist's life trying to distract her from her life's work and making art seem like an impractical vocation. Creativity takes a lot of courage, because it is a process that takes time, skill, effort and development and it cannot be rushed. Being an artist is not an instantly rewarding profession. Being an artist is a person saying to oneself, 'I have a right to be me and I have a right to do what I love. In time I will be rewarded: maybe financially, maybe otherwise, but I will not give up on who I am.'

Creativity is about bringing forth something that doesn't exist, yet it is a sacred process. It needs to happen in a safe environment where the artist feels free to create and to be herself. This doesn't always happen in art schools – especially in ones where criticism is a strong force. Creativity is not forceful, it is an unfolding of the feelings that an artist has towards the subject matter that she is painting. It takes some separation and skills of detaching from those who think that they can control an artist with criticism. Envy can be vicious. This is why self-awareness as well as awareness of the weaknesses of others can be a great asset. In time, it is probably best to empty one's life of those who are unconstructive. There are many positive people who enjoy good art and who value an artist's labour of love.

Sometimes the rigour of an art course can motivate one to go to the galleries and draw and at other times one needs to do this for oneself. Doing this simply for the benefit of it can be very rewarding, even though I really prefer to be in my studio drawing and painting my own subject matter. But I know from my study of artists that all the best ones copied other great artists to develop their work.

CREATIVE FLAIR

This is how we learn. Copying is a discipline that helps us to concentrate and think about the ideas of other artists. When I've copied from paintings in the National Gallery, apart from tuning into my own thoughts as I was working in a meditative way, I was also thinking about the subject matter and the artist's choice of describing it. We all see things in our individual way and sometimes we learn best how others see things by copying from their work. We do this not slavishly, but with an aim to bring our own creative flair to the simple work of copying. We can challenge ourselves to still maintain our originality even as we 'dialogue' with another artist.

When we are no longer in art school we don't have others to tell us what we are doing wrong or right according to them. It gives us time and space to hear our own thoughts about the work we are doing. Because of my work with children and my awareness of my own sensitivity to criticism, I know that I need to go easy on myself. Every work of art is a stepping-stone in practising my craft. Like a child, I feel really happy every time I am creative and usually I like my latest work the best. However, sometimes when I review what I've done so far, I marvel at some of my earlier works and the freedom I felt with that particular work. I think many artists are perfectionists and this is actually a good thing, in my opinion, for artists as we do our work. This is not to say that my work is perfect, but I do aim to do my best with each one. This is what makes me happy: to do my best and to know that I am working with the talent that I have been given.

Painting gives me the unique opportunity to please myself. I usually don't even think about whether it will please someone else until I show it to them. This is another beauty of art. It creates a window of freedom in my life through which my idealism can fly freely like a dove. I find this very precious. This is what brings me to my easel with a sense of purpose; this is what makes my heart sing with joy as I squeeze out my colours and apply them to the canvas. There is a burst of fun each time I paint. The practice of mixing colour in new ways to create a harmonious effect is one of the main reasons that I paint. Harmony is important to me because it relaxes my mind and channels my thoughts towards a sense of peace.

TOOLS AND RESOURCES

The canvas, colours and the paintbrush are an artist's basic tools. I don't think it matters too much whether you are set up at home or in the studio, as long as you have a sense of space and freedom the world is your oyster. I had just as much fun creating in my home as I now do in my studio. In fact, when I just have my dining room table I am very creative with the use of colour in the background. So, each set up has its own challenges and assets.

An artist generates her creativity from within but needs the impetus from the world around her. Regular time spent in nature and in looking at good quality art feeds the need for images. We rely on the language of images to do our work well. It's rewarding to go to an art gallery, such as the Courtauld Gallery in London, and to see how playfully modern artists like the Fauves and the Impressionists used and played with colour to manipulate the scenery that they painted. The playfulness can be very liberating when one is trying too hard with something. After all, it's only art! I say that but of course art can be very demanding.

I think it's good for artists to be in touch with the creativity of others around us and see how others use this beautiful gift. Going to see dancers, listening to our favourite musicians, being open to others, reading poetry filled with metaphor and imagery, can do us a world of good. Other gifts float into our lives. One such gift for me was the book *The Language of Flowers*, a romance novel by the author Vanessa Diffenbaugh. Being a painter of flowers, it really spoke to my heart and made me think about what I am communicating with my work and my choice of subject matter. I imagine that in your life you have also had many such similar experiences. The world is full of talented people who are using their skills and knowledge to brighten people's lives, to give hope and to inspire.

EXPANDING

As we practice, we expand our interests and horizons. New things start to come into our lives and to vie for our attention. What's important and what matters needs to be gauged against our priorities. As we develop our work, we begin to be more conscious about how and with whom we spend our time. We really don't want to waste our resources with things and with people who bring us down or undermine our work and creative efforts. Creative people can often be very generous and want the best for everyone. This is wonderful as long as it is a two-way exchange.

It can be very draining, for example, to be supportive and encouraging towards someone who just takes that energy but doesn't offer something similar back. Energy needs to be rewarded for energy. Love for love. Attention for attention. Kindness for kindness. Otherwise what is the point? We cannot rescue everyone.

Looking at things from this perspective we can see the value of practising our craft as a mirror that reflects back honestly who we are. If we can see clearly and plainly that we are people who deserve our respect, because we are honest towards our work, then it goes to show that those who do not mirror this respect back to us don't value us. This can be unpleasant, but this is also a part of reality. We can lie and pretend that everyone loves us, but we know better. We will have our friends and we will have those whom we prefer not to spend time with. *C'est la vie!* We may, at times, get ourselves hurt, but we recover and put another foot forward on our path. By now it needs to be clear that art is our path. It may be a winding road, but it is the friendliest road we can take if we want to be fulfilled as artists.

So – what were you born to paint? I think back now with much fondness towards the great painter Van Gogh. He was born to paint his sunflowers and his swirling stars. The joy that radiates from his yellow sunflowers that are so full of character they are almost human is wonderful to behold. I think it's especially lovely that he originally painted them as a gift to his then friend Gaugain. It shows the power of his heart and the depths of his love – what more can an artist do with his work than this? His purpose to please his friend and make his arrival welcoming is moving.

It's very sad that he didn't live to see his work valued and appreciated by the rest of the world. Luckily for us artists he remains an inspiration with his thick use of paint, bold colours and original subject matters. He practised incessantly, almost obsessively. His was a unique temperament and his letters revealed that he himself did not think that he would have a long life; perhaps this was the cause of his sense of urgency. All the same, he leaves behind a great legacy and his artwork is forever worthy of admiration and praise.

LIVING WELL

I singled out Van Gogh because for me he is one of the greatest painters ever, but I like to think that his life also cautions other artists to look after themselves and to take care of all aspects of their being. We want to be healthy and we want to keep living. Ideally, we want to make a living! I am sure if Van Gogh paid me a visit he would encourage me to keep painting what I love but to find a way to make my art pay. I know that he suffered from adverse feelings of being dependent on his brother

Theo, but who knows if things could have been any different for him. Anyhow, I like to think that his spirit lives on and that he is encouraged by the impact that he had on the lives of many artists as well as the general public who love his work.

When one's heart is into one's work there is a synergy that makes it all worthwhile. Wherever we practice our craft, if we work with the intention to fulfil our destinies as artists we are being successful. Images feed the soul in a way that words cannot. Sometimes an image is so powerful that its message can heal or liberate a suffering soul. I am not a psychotherapist, but I have taken some classes in art therapy and I have also read about its positive effects. In my life I was feeling out of sorts about something one day and as I walked into a gallery a small picture caught my eye. It was a painting of a deer running up a mountain looking up at a little bird in the air. The title of the painting was *In difficult times*. I felt an enormous sense of relief and the message of that painting has stayed with me today. I found it very encouraging and I still feel grateful for the way that it resonated with how I was feeling at the time.

For me this goes to show that even though we often work in isolation, there is a God who takes care of his artists and makes sure that they are okay. The signs may be small and quiet, but as long as we stay open and receptive to them we will notice them and feel their benefit. For me, the best remedy for when an artist feels alone is to walk into an art gallery with great art and feel among friends. We are all part of the history of the lives of the artists, whatever the size or the subject matter of our work.

OUR TRIBE

We may not all make it into the hall of fame and in many instances, this is not even desirable, but we are among the creative tribe of painters. It's best to know and acknowledge this so that we can comfort ourselves and have a wider perspective on things. This is especially useful when we feel hurt, confused or alone. Many have gone before us and have experienced similar things. Also, many of our feelings are just there because we are human, and it comes with the deal.

Practice of art alternated with resting makes for a more balanced kind of existence. It is the being and the doing, the ying and the yang, the feminine and the masculine, and the general tension and balancing out of the opposites within ourselves. Without practice we can feel aimless and without rest we can feel stressed. Being aimless or stressed does not serve our art, or our wellbeing, either physically or mentally. The joy of practising and the serenity of rest harmonises the tensions inherent to the creative temperament and makes our lives flow a little easier. Whatever we can do to make ourselves happy we need to do. In my experience, when I practice my painting and drawing I feel fulfilled and when I rest I feel I good, knowing that

I will be in a better mental and emotional position to start my work afresh.

Improving our work happens only with practice. We cannot dream of images that we hope to realise if we do not paint them or draw them. The creation of images and pictures happens most naturally when we are fully active in our work. We can be active both at work and at rest. I don't know if an artist's mind can ever fully disengage, but maybe that isn't entirely necessary. When we bring our feelings into the paintings, we are animating our work and creating things that can stir the heart and feed the soul. This is the value of practice.

CHAPTER 6

ENJOYMENT - LIBERATING THE SOUL

The soul of the child needs love, praise and encouragement. This is what is felt as warmth. When I worked with children aged five and under, their little size did not hide their big personalities and especially their need to be creative and to be loved. They absorbed appreciation, not just for what they made but for who they were. On one occasion in a Montessori nursery, I went over to play with a little blonde-haired girl with sparkly blue eyes. She was very busy building something with the wooden blocks. She acknowledged my presence and we chatted briefly, but she was so absorbed in what she was doing that I just sat there silently watching her. I did not want to intrude and disturb her concentration. All of a sudden, she looked up at me and said these words, which I will never forget: 'I am going to show you something you have never seen before!' I was enchanted. She was three years old. Clearly, she knew the originality of her work – her unique creation.

On another occasion, after I stopped working with children and was working as an artist, I was coming up the escalator in the underground. In front of me was a young black girl about eight years old. She was admiring something that she was holding in her hands. It was something she had made at school. I consider being friendly to children one of my joys, as well as my way of having fun, so I asked her if I could see what she had created. I looked at it and though I couldn't exactly tell what it was, something about it looked different. 'I think you are very clever,' I said. She replied without missing a beat, 'I know, the others just did bows.' She spoke like a true artist, I thought. She knew that what she had made was distinctive from what the others had made, and she had great confidence in this.

The creative spark in a child is tender. It needs to be nurtured and encouraged. Some adults might be more resilient, but no matter what the outer performance is, in my observation anyone can be affected by someone else's insensitivity or, at times, downright cruelty. I think the answer is to become very confident in one's own creative work as well as in one's own sense of self. This may take some time.

We are social beings, so we often take cues from other people. This is especially true if one is sensitive to other people. However, it is worth becoming even more sensitive to ourselves and listening to our own hearts. When we listen to ourselves we ask the questions that matter to us and we get the answers that make a difference to us. When we ask other people, or listen to their answers, we get their version of 'life.'

LISTENING WITHIN

Since no two people have the same personality, let alone character, we cannot give the reigns of responsibility to other people without feeling that somehow we are going against our own nature. Of course, we can talk to people and listen to what they have to say, but we are wise when we leave plenty of room to make up our own minds and come to our own decisions. I know that this is easier said than done sometimes, but I think that when I consider this for myself, in the present and in the future, this will always make sense to me.

I have made the mistake of taking action because someone else said so and I have regretted it. For example, before I was clear that I wanted to be an artist, I accepted someone's advice to just take 'any job.' So 'any job' became working on reception. This was after years of study. I hated the job so much and I was constantly missing something. As I said to someone at the time, 'I miss beauty.'

That should have been my clue! For me, beauty equals art and being creative. I experienced no joy doing an administrative job that did not make use of my artistic talents and where every day was the same with the same joyless routine. It took some time and listening to other people's suggestions and getting 'it' wrong again and again before I finally decided that enough was enough and I was going to do what I am good at.

It's so easy to take our talents for granted. Oh yes, we

think anyone can draw and colour, but we know that this is not so. I like to think that everyone is good at something and they can be creative in that something, whether it is working with money or working with people or animals or what have you, but no two people are good at the same thing in exactly the same way. And here is the gem of the puzzle piece: your heart is the centre of love and creativity. It tells you exactly what you need to be doing at the time that you are ready to finally listen to it and let go of what everyone else is telling you to do. If you have bossy and controlling people in your life who tell you what you should be doing all the time, it can be difficult to hear your own voice.

But your own voice will not let you down, whereas their voices will. Their voices do not flow from your heart – they flow from theirs. Very often, controlling people have no insight into another's problems because they are so focused on themselves and their opinions, which they naturally consider most important and relevant to your life. This is why spending time alone – often in nature – will yield dividends in learning to listen to your own heart and honestly follow its guidance.

God cares about your life and he cares about you. Each creature is entirely unique in design and what you love to do belongs to you. Don't let other people take away what you are here to do. They can't really, but it can feel like that if you listen to others. Over time, as we get to know other people a bit better, we may become especially careful about who we can trust with our dreams.

OUR DREAMS

Our dreams are precious, and they are not to be thrown to people without discernment. They have been given to us to discover, to nurture and to bring to life. What is lying dormant in us is waiting to be awakened and we come alive as we give our dreams wings and do things that we truly enjoy. We all love to feel good and when we make feeling good our priority the other things fall by the wayside more easily. Who cares what an intrusive person has to say about our life? They may just be blowing hot air and we need not inhale it.

We can really find a lot of good things inside ourselves when we take the time to look. We can encourage ourselves, we can praise ourselves, we can be there for ourselves when things get tough, we can challenge ourselves and we can continue to strive to be excellent in all that we are and all that we do. Nobody needs to come and tell us how to be or what to do. In fact, as we engage with ourselves in more and more positive and supportive ways, we may gradually grow very bored with external forces pushing and pulling us. Hopefully, we start getting a sense of our own purpose or if we haven't worked that one out yet, we can trust that we are on our way.

When we do what we love, we derive a sense of simple

enjoyment from almost everything about our life. We appreciate the little things like a child smiling at us, a hot drink on a cold day, the warmth of the sunshine, the changing colours of the evening sky, and we generally start to connect to the natural world effortlessly. Even if we are not a 'somebody' in the eyes of the world, we begin to feel like a 'somebody' to ourselves because we are being true to who and what we are. We are shaping our lives from within, we are painting our own self-image onto the canvas. What we are creating is not just a body of work but the work of our soul.

OUR WORK - OUR SOUL

It can be difficult for some artists to part from their paintings and to sell them. They feel like our creative babies. We have poured our love, our life and our spirit into them. We know the effort and will that it took to create them – it is not an easy process to put a price tag on all that. For that reason, it can be most reassuring to sell the paintings to nice people, knowing that they are going to good homes where they will be appreciated.

I think our work can teach us to be good to ourselves. It does this by reflecting back to us the quality of our labour and the care we have taken in painting a picture. Whatever we take care of, takes care of us. If we keep our studios clean and tidy, we will be able to do better work than if we are working in a clutter-filled environment. We do things well when we make things easier for ourselves. To concentrate and focus we need space and the overall sense that everything we need is in place and whatever we don't need is well out of sight.

This can be a metaphor for the rest of our lives as well. Whether you are someone who can multi-task or focus on only one thing at a time, you still need to set things up to serve your needs and your best interests. We all know intuitively what things and people support us, as well as what and who do not.

On a course in positive psychology I learned a skill that has definitely added to my sense of enjoyment about my life. Every evening I write down three good things that have happened during the day into a small notebook. There may have been many more, and often there are, but writing down three helps me to really focus on what pleased me the most. This helps to eliminate the negative and accentuate the positive.

Doing this over a period of time is a good way to see on paper what brings me joy and makes my life good. Doing more of what we like is key to enjoyment. We were taught to try and record three novel things each day, so it is not a repetitive list but something that surprises us. I recommend this exercise if you are feeling stuck in some way or just thinking that there is nothing good in your life at the moment. If you take a look, there is always something that you can find. Looking for the good can be a useful guide out of a bad situation. If the idea pleases you try it and see what happens.

CHILDREN AND MY TRUE 'SELF'

Although I did not enjoy teaching very much as I didn't feel that it was my purpose in life, I did enjoy being with little children immensely. They were super cute and a lot of fun. For me, they are what the daffodils were to Wordsworth. In my moments of solitude, I often think back to my conversations with them and I smile or laugh out loud, remembering their sweetness or their astute insight into something. I never get tired of such memories! I hope that one day should any of 'my' little children read this, they will know, if they didn't already, how much I valued them and how much I loved being with them.

I loved how their feelings would sit on their faces and I could tell whether they were cross or happy. Their faces would show the moment's 'weather report' of mood and the emotion would either pass or be expressed in a very clear and direct way. Whilst I did have to ask what was going on for them, I didn't have to guess. Often, I heard it immediately. For example, on one occasion I got angry with a little boy (aged four). He looked up at me with hurt and confusion in his eyes and said, 'I don't like it when you get cross with me.' I apologised and explained why I was angry. Soon we were friends again – his hurt was appeased, and my anger evaporated.

I learned so much from children about how to be natural. I think I was always that way inside but because of past hurts I had hidden my true self. This was especially true when I wasn't an artist. When I was on my life-coaching course with a room full of business types I became very aware of this. I didn't feel very comfortable in the group and I didn't feel that I fitted in. We were doing a coaching session and I mentioned that I didn't feel that I could really say that I was a 'coach.' The person coaching me looked at me and dismissively asked me, 'Well, if you are not a coach then what are you?' Exactly. I am an artist. I regard coaching as a natural human activity; at one time or another we have all coached somebody, but to be an artist, at least for me, makes me feel like the real me.

It is to this identity that I dedicate this body of work. Not just for myself but for any artist struggling with their sense of self. As artists we can often stick out for not being like everyone else. This can be confusing and difficult to bear at times. We all have a need to belong and to feel like we are part of the human family. It is my prayer that we all find a happy circle that we can feel appreciated in. We are all alone until we find that through hard work, talent, imagination and love we are brought among the fold that is ours.

Until we find this sense of belonging, we may need to rely on the resources that we have. Reading good books that speak to us is one way and doing our work is another way. The subject matter – in my case flowers – can be a source of pleasure and comfort as well. I get to do what I love, and the canvas reflects this love back to me. The joy of art is that the results are visible. This is why I previously mentioned that if you are feeling stuck or sad, even making one mark can be a way forwards and out of that difficulty you are facing.

HEALING THE SOUL

Making marks and colouring is beautiful work for the soul. The sense of liberty and ownership that it gives makes it well worthwhile. When we are being true to ourselves and to who we are – that is artists – we begin to walk to that 'distant drummer.' We may even become pioneers in our own lives. We are no longer at the mercy of the sirens around, but we become the captain of our own ship and we can sail to distant and undiscovered lands.

We are rich with possibilities and it is up to us to discover these riches within ourselves. If we feel like we are mysteries to ourselves that can be a good thing, because mysteries are there to be unravelled. It is good to take along a good author who is an excellent guide and personally I don't know of anyone better than the Swiss psychiatrist and psychotherapist, Carl Jung.

Having faith in God is especially helpful because with him we feel less alone. Whatever it is or whoever it is that speaks to your soul in the way that you hear best, I encourage you to make the most of them. Being on good terms with ourselves and having a sense of peace about what we are doing lights up our inner light and brings a sparkle to our eyes. Maybe one day we will say to someone what that little girl said to me, 'I am going to show you something you have never seen before!' And that, to me, is the essence of being an artist.

CHAPTER 7

QUIET – THE BEAUTY OF GOING WITHIN

It is in the quiet moments of our days that we can tune into our hearts and what they are saying. It is very difficult, in fact virtually impossible, to listen to ourselves amidst noise. Quiet and noise are so opposite in their effect on us. The former encourages reflection and often honesty with how we truly are, and the latter takes up our energy and diverts our attention from ourselves. So really it is being quiet that centres our minds and lets us be who we are. We need the stillness to feel relaxed enough to make the decisions that most benefit us.

Have you ever felt conflicted in making a decision? I think all of us have at some point. For some of us making decisions can be very automatic, but when we give ourselves time and space to think things through we can make wiser decisions. Some decisions are minor, but others can have longer lasting consequences. Thankfully, many things can be changed or altered and even reversed, but it is still good practice to allow for moments of peace and quiet to get clear about what we want to do.

For artists being quiet is especially important. It is in this state that we receive our ideas and recharge our creativity. I recognise the process for what it is and (usually) I don't try to force things to happen. Being quiet and listening to myself is teaching me to be patient and let things unfold in their own time. Being human, and somewhat impatient and impulsive by temperament, I need to practice this daily. And I do this with meditation.

Meditation is very gentle and very powerful. The form that you chose to use is up to you. I find sitting still and repeating a simple word as a mantra quietly to myself the most beneficial. This way I am listening to my own thoughts and observing my own feelings. Having said that, I have also loved and benefited from guided meditations, though I tend to use these only occasionally. I heartily recommend trying out a few things, experimenting and see what works for you. Whatever calms you down, makes you feel relaxed and more centred is best.

Quiet is a simple word, but even just focusing on it brings a kind of gentle power into play. In this state there is an absence of control, of force, of negativity or even emptiness. Being quiet can be a very active and receptive state. Being receptive is not easy for everyone. Receiving love, receiving appreciation and receiving thanks can be more difficult if we are used to being giving or controlling. When we are receiving we are allowing nice feelings to arise in us and make us feel good. Being receptive is becoming open to all kinds of experiences and sometimes we need to filter out what is beneficial to us and what is not.

Learning to attract things just by simply being ourselves is an art in itself, in which meditation has a profound role to play. We have all heard of the law of attraction and some books explain it better than others. I am not an expert in this area, but any of us can observe through experience and awareness the things and people that we are attracted to. What do they look like? How do they behave? What attracts us to them? Pondering questions like these may help to see what in us is attractive to other people. It can be useful to consider whether we are happy with the things and people who we are attracting. If we are not then we may need to make small adjustments and give out clearer signals and messages about what we like and accept and what we do not.

ATTRACTING BEAUTY

Flowers attract life to them. Bees love them. People love them. They are inherently attractive. This simple example may give us clues about the nature of attraction. We all attract and repel. When we acknowledge this, we can take care of ourselves a little better. Artists really need to take care of themselves because being creative generally comes with a heightened sense of sensitivity and openness. Of course we are all different, but it is worth really spending time and attention to learn to take excellent care of ourselves. How we do this is not prescriptive and often involves trial and error and learning from our mistakes, as well as from what works for us. Being able to be quiet is a very practical way to enhance this skill.

Many of us have a need to process things, events and people, and simply to be. Perhaps this applies more to people who are introverted and draw their energy from within but at times this need is felt by all of us. Otherwise we are just charging through life, one activity after another, without the space and time (not to mention care) to appreciate what is happening and what we are doing with ourselves and in our relationships. Again, on this matter we are all our own experts. What works for one person will vary from what works for another.

This is an invitation to consider the many benefits of slowing down and stopping once in a while. If we are always on the go, this is especially important. Otherwise we may be forced to slow down either by some form of illness (if we haven't been listening to our bodies) or something in our relationships will go amiss to tell us to turn inwards a bit and see what we need to be doing.

For me, it has been of immense benefit to have a room of my own just for me and me alone. It really gives me the mind space to create exactly as I like in my own way and I am very grateful for it. Artists need space to create. It is best when it is suited to them and their personalities. I hope that if you are an artist reading this and you haven't yet got one, that one day you will have the place of your dreams! Until you do, it is still good to create moments of stillness to help your creativity and give your heart a chance to speak to you.

A QUIET MIND

Images arise when the mind is quiet. Like birds they take flight in our minds and once free they have been released into existence and it then becomes our privilege to put them down on the canvas. We may have dreamt up something in our quiet time that we would never have dreamt up in a noisy atmosphere. This is the value of stillness. Quiet opens a window in our imaginations so that the sun can shine in and light up our thoughts and feelings. Together our thoughts and feelings become like dance partners, each influencing the other in the sequence of their steps, guiding us to a vision of beauty.

In this act of listening within, we become more self-directed and this will pave the way for our vision of beauty to emerge and continue to grow and blossom forever. I like to say forever, because if we tend to a quieter mind, our mind will reward us with what we need as artists. Our heart will then be happy to communicate with us because she knows that we are listening to her. Being creative heals our hearts beautifully. In giving form, and infusing that special form with colour, we light up our senses and bring a sense of excitement and inner peace.

Many of us have experienced our hearts being in conflict with our head, but creativity bridges that gap because it is the language of the soul. The soul is eternal and is inherently free, or wants to be, and creativity can be a helpful agent in helping it become liberated.

Creativity may not save us entirely from all the pain and trials of life, but it can help us make sense of them, give shape to them and above all, express them. This expression is so powerful that this alone makes doing art worthwhile. It takes a lot of energy not to express feelings and it takes courage to express them. When we paint our feelings into our art we are communicating with a language that goes beyond what words can say.

Pictures and images come from the unconscious, and for this they are to be respected. This is especially true if the artist has learned her craft and is applying conscious skill to the vision that comes from somewhere deep inside. It is a kind of mystery to paint because the process engages us on so many levels, yet the results often look simple and effortless. Doing things that come naturally is the best way to be as an artist. If one doesn't enjoy the subject matter, it is best to find another until it fits with your personality, values and your vision.

HAVING A VISION

What is it that you wish to communicate with your art? Asking yourself this simple question will shape your journey in this life as an artist. For example, I paint colourful pictures of flowers because I want to communicate my love for their beauty, colour and form. This is very simplistic – of course I want to achieve a lot more with my work. I want my paintings to bring people a sense of peace, harmony and joy when they look at my work. These are the qualities that I value about art and I also feel strongly that art should communicate an artist's love for the subject she paints. Without the special light of love, an artwork simply looks lifeless and art needs to be about life and colour and hope, to my way of thinking.

Many artists love to put their thoughts down in writing and do it quite well. Perhaps you do too. Maybe you like to compose little poems or enjoy writing in your journal. Whatever form of writing we love to do, we need to keep doing it. Writing is an excellent way to process our thinking and get clarity about our feelings about things.

Like meditation, it is another way of being quiet and listening to what really matters to us most. Sometimes we really don't know these things unless we take the trouble to sit down and do them. So often I have resisted writing in my journal and then ended up feeling like a boiling pot of water with a lid on it. As soon as I sit down to write and allow my feelings to come through,

I gain insight, understanding and, at times, even make some good decisions that I probably would not have made had I not done it.

WRITING THINGS DOWN

We are so full of passions and desires, and feelings can be very strong, taking us in different directions. Writing gives us that opportunity to explore these different currents and not get carried away by any of them. Like a roomful of noisy and excited little children, our feelings tell us different things and as we let the words flow we slowly start to feel more in control and less likely to be pushed or pulled in the wrong direction. Writing can strengthen us in listening to our own voice. Of course, sometimes just talking about our feelings can be helpful but others may not always be available whereas a journal always is. It is a question of choice and sometimes just doing it, even when we resist it, can be more helpful than we ever thought possible.

If I get very strong feelings about something I like to write little poems that sum up simply and concisely how I am feeling inside. This offers relief and release from the tension that is inside me and I am free to move on. Whether we are painting or writing, the expression of ideas is given shape. An artist will often have many creative ideas and being quiet and still can help us focus on just one. The rest of the ideas can be written down or let go of naturally. There is action and inaction (being receptive) in the creative process and learning to engage with both is part of the process.

The messages of the heart often come through quietly. Have you had the experience of meeting a person and getting a feeling about them? Well, this is a quiet bodily sensation telling you what is going on inside you, even if appearances are giving you different information. This sense of intuition is your guiding light. Of course, the more you practice being aware of your inner state and checking it out with reality, the better position you will have of acting in your own best interest. Being guided by one's heart is a journey par excellence because it is a more scenic route through life. When reason alone rules, we are out of touch with what really matters to us, and in the affairs of the heart we become out of shape. Becoming still helps us exercise this attentiveness to our feelings and we can become better agents to our true self.

Learning to love quiet things in a world often filled with noise and over-stimulation of the senses is very worthwhile. We will less likely be followers of the herd and more in touch with what we want and have the courage to go after it. We may know what we want but having the courage to pursue it is something else. Courage can be built up in stillness of mind. When we have nothing better to do than to wait on our 'self' we will inevitably, sooner or later, come up with the solution to our own problem. Just like a little child needs patience, our inner self needs patience.

LEARNING TO WAIT

How can anyone make their minds up if one feels it has to be done in a hurry? This can be very stressful. To avoid this stress, we learn to wait. It isn't easy but at the same time it is very simple. We can go about our daily activities even as we wait to hear from our heart when she is ready to tell us what we need to hear.

If we are honest, sometimes we don't want to hear certain things. This may be the reason we have ignored our heart, our feelings and our intuition. We may not want to hear that we need to quit our job or end a relationship or move homes. We are aware of the difficulties of change and change can create stress. I don't know about you, but change is not my area of specialty. I resist it fiercely. I am not proud of this, it is just the way it is with me.

I like to be 'sure' and 'certain' before I leap and if I could have it, I would want a crystal ball to show me what that will look like in full colour. Since this is not going to happen, I struggle with the feelings change brings up for me. If I could have it my way – well – things would just stay the same. Except they don't, and my resistance brings up its own difficulties.

So how is being quiet and still a way to solve our problems and our difficulties with things like change? It is something that we all have to answer for ourselves. For me, it is a way of coping and becoming aware of my own needs rather than being at the mercy of what others would have me do. By becoming more centred and focused I am less likely to toss in the waves of indecision forever. I imagine this is true for you as well. If you are a very decisive person and have no problems with change this might not apply to you directly but for those of us who do, being quiet is essential.

Spending time listening to ourselves is not wasted in the long run. We may find that we develop a more gentle, compassionate and kind attitude to ourselves and in doing so we become better decision makers. Our identity – our sense of self – can then be more flexible, rather than rigid, and we may find that we become open to new possibilities and we begin to see good things on the horizon for us. As artists and as people the self-knowledge and self-love we can gain in moments of quiet become our wisest teachers in life. Who knows, we might even become better painters!

CHAPTER 8

SOLITUDE – WHERE THE INNER STRENGTH LIES

This is probably the most challenging and difficult chapter to write for me so far. I am thinking that unless I use some specific examples from my own life to illustrate my point, I will miss the mark. So, this will mean re-visiting one of the most difficult and recent experiences that I had which put me on a steep learning curve about myself and other people.

Loneliness is very painful whereas solitude is good for the soul. Feeling lonely can even be physically painful, not just psychologically. On the other hand, solitude can be very productive and can enhance one's self-knowledge and awareness of one's own needs and how to best meet them. I imagine that I am not alone in having experienced both states. I am a person who needs solitude, but I don't like to feel lonely. When I feel lonely I need to switch to activities that put me back in touch with myself, such as going swimming, going for a walk in nature or simply listening to music. Elvis works every time! Excellent rock and roll does wonders for my soul.

Simply taking care of the next thing that is in front of me keeps the rhythm of life going and I can snap out of feeling sad about feeling lonely. It might be that I need to clean the house or do my shopping. Paying attention to the small things can be very effective in combatting a sense of isolation. Isolation sometimes comes with the territory of being an artist, though not necessarily. I remind myself that having faith in what I am doing and my purpose in doing it will eventually lead me into having a much fuller and more meaningful life. Existential questions are best left for journaling. That doesn't mean that they cease to exist, but it means that they are being acknowledged on paper and given a voice.

I don't think that the meaning of my whole life is making art. For me art is the best way I know how to express my creative spirit and to create a kind of beauty that is most special to me. I have other hopes and ambitions for my life, which I am working towards. Just as I write these words, two magpies have perched themselves on top of the building block where I live. They appear to be kissing. This image is fitting because in my heart of hearts I believe that the whole beauty of existence is to love and be loved. I almost think of art as a prelude to this grander play.

Any kind of work that one is dedicated to is excellent preparation for sharing one's life. This is so, I believe, because by coming to know and use one's talents one is in a much stronger position to appreciate the true self.

It is from *this* self that we are able then to choose the person who is right for us.

DEEPER DISCOVERY

This journey of getting to know ourselves, discovering and using our talents, can sometimes be a process filled with trial and error, heartache and disappointment. Even when we are doing something that we love, we are still not immune from the daily vicissitudes of life but we are in a better position to integrate our experiences into our work. This happened in a very direct way for me when I decided to train as a life coach.

One of my dreams was to help people. I consider myself to be caring and empathic and I love to be of help if I can, and if someone lets me. I signed up for a training course full of hope and expectations. I thought at the time that I could combine being an artist with being a life coach. What a beautiful marriage of my talents! So, I was buzzing with excitement about all that I would learn and be able to put into practice.

The course was organised so that we worked in pairs in between our training sessions. This all went well until things went wrong for me. I get a sinking sensation just remembering these events. I approached somebody to be my coach who reminded me (at least physically) of a coach I had once worked with. The person who chose me must have had his own reasons, though to this day

I am not sure what they were, for working with me, though I have some idea.

I will call the person who coached me Suzette and the person I was coaching Lucy. I had a good first session with Suzette, so I began to feel a sense of trust. My coaching session with Lucy was a bit more disturbing, though I couldn't put my finger at first on what it was about her that was beginning to make me feel dread in coaching her again. All the same I persisted with both, not considering that I might actually have the choice to opt out if I wanted to. I was just focused on fulfilling the necessary requirements to pass the course.

The last coaching session with Suzette went completely wrong for me. I opened up my feelings about some feedback that I had received on the course, which left me feeling uncertain. With a person like Suzette this proved to be a mistake. She was not what I would call a compassionate or empathic person. Instead, she used my vulnerability to attack me. She told me that I had thin skin and that I should get a thicker one. And so on. I was shocked. Her vehemence also took me by surprise. Let's just say, Suzette was not a 'safe' person, an individual to whom one can be open with one's feelings. I learned this the hard way.

Coaching Lucy turned into a big challenge. She turned out to be emotionally abusive. She was constantly disrespectful and was spiteful. I was having a very bad coaching experience. Because I was so new to the world of coaching, I went in there completely open to the experience I would have. I was not warned, I didn't prepare myself and I was not as cautious as I might be today.

Both of these experiences were very damaging at the time. Because of my sensitivity to criticism, which I mentioned earlier, I was, for a while, in a very dark place that I wasn't sure how to get out of. Today I would not work with such individuals out of a sense of self-preservation but at the time I persevered. However, the steep learning curve that I mentioned earlier began for me.

LEARNING FROM EXPERIENCE

I was not happy to leave myself in such a barren emotional place. I wanted to understand better why I had been so adversely affected and what I could do to prevent it in the future. I had to accept and swallow one difficult pill that had caused me much joy but also much pain in my life as well: I am very sensitive. If truth be told, I used to hate this quality about myself because as I was growing up this quality was often met with ridicule and derision. No wonder I was sensitive to being sensitive! Every time someone would call me 'sensitive' in a hurtful way, I felt like there was something wrong with me. Someone to be rejected, not loved and appreciated. It seems I have been meeting many of the wrong kind of people.

So, I decided to take action. I decided that I was going to learn all that I can about this quality which a part of me secretly admired and valued about myself and I would find a therapist who could help me heal from these inflicted wounds. So I did and I have. I am writing about these painful experiences because I know that there are many artists out there who are very sensitive. It often comes with the territory and we need to learn both to protect ourselves and to be able to choose safe people to be with who value our inherent nature. I also recognise that there are many artists for whom this is not a hot or burning issue and they have felt loved and accepted for who they are all their lives. So, this story and its moral is more for those of us who have suffered because of not valuing this trait in ourselves.

Coming to value our sensitivity is not an easy process. We can read a book like *The Highly Sensitive Person* and feel really good about who we are and having this humane trait, only to come across some insensitive person (I am talking about bullies, not the occasional insensitivity which to a degree we all possess at times) and feel hurt 'again.' I wish I had a magic wand to wave over every hurt so I can recover faster and not suffer.

I do think that the suffering does lessen, and we grow wiser about how best to defend ourselves and protect ourselves. Sometimes we may even have to go on the offensive and confront – again there is an art to this for sensitive people who typically hate confrontations. Avoiding a bully or telling them to back off might well be necessary at times. Each situation will be different.

EVALUATING OTHERS

It might be worth mentioning that although there are many lovely people, there are quite a few unhealthy people as well. We all get to decide who is unhealthy for us, according to our own definition. Narcissistic people are inherently unhealthy and 'bad' for us and are best to keep away from. Other than the obvious ones, there are also the subtler ones: people you don't feel that you can trust on some level, people who betray your confidence in them, people who lie, people who are disrespectful towards us and so on. The list might be long or short, depending on your life experience and what you are willing to accept.

Solitude can be a wonderful teacher. When we are peacefully alone we have the time to reflect on the life we are leading, and we can see where we need to keep learning and where we are doing very well. The above example of a difficulty that I had, has yielded many positive results that have me led me to making healthier choices for myself about who I let in. Of course, for a while we may feel like we want to keep everyone out until we 'heal' and that is fine. But whilst we suffer in a relationship, we also recover in a healthy one.

For every person who behaves badly there is a really good person who can help us recover and be true to our self and our life's aim. We do need to keep in mind that we have goals that we want to achieve and over time we learn that it is necessary to keep our eyes on the ball.

An artist's eye is best kept on making art and taking care of herself.

I recently read an excellent business book by Jonathan Rees called *Do Protect*. His central theme is about making sure that we protect our business and he looks at the different areas in setting up a business that need this kind of special attention. This is a good time to underline the implicit need to protect ourselves, not just in business but also as individuals, especially so when we are sensitive. Our gifts and time are precious, and we can learn to be choosy about whom we bestow our energy on.

SENSITIVITY

The good thing about being very sensitive, or finely tuned as I often like to think of it, is that we are highly self-aware. We just need to balance this out by becoming more aware of other people and their motives. I know that we are very good at picking up their energy, feelings and moods, but we can also trust our intuition about them. Rather than focus, for example, on whether a particular person likes us, we can ask instead: how do I feel in this person's company? Good? Bad? Indifferent? And then actually listen to what the answers are and take action on them.

Perhaps we have ignored our intuition in the past and put up with people and situations that haven't served our best interest. Our best interest is to make sure that, as much as possible, we feel good and we feel well in ourselves. On the next occasion when someone crosses our path we need to tune into that little voice inside us that tells us what is going on in our interaction with this person. I know that we often like to feel that people deserve a second chance. This is correct. I have been given many second chances in my life and I am very grateful for them because they allowed me to progress and grow as a person. But we get to decide. If a person definitely feels wrong, then they are wrong for us and we can move on.

Sometimes fear keeps us stuck in a relationship or in a situation. I know this is true and has been true for myself in several instances when it was really time to let go and to move on. I am not comfortable with letting go and if I don't see clearly where or how I can move on. I hold back. This isn't helpful because it keeps the situation as a status quo.

I don't know about you, but I usually need to move through something to let go unless it's a very simple decision and the steps are clear. In more difficult cases I need to have a deep understanding and I need to keep building enough trust in myself that I know that I will be alright if and when I make the decision to let go. I need to light up the situation from all angles, consider my options and then choose the one that best suits my personality. I need to be keenly aware of my own feelings. Fear can be a very big block and I need a steady dose of faith to move through it.

ENDINGS

This is especially true when it means ending a close relationship that is no longer healthy. The reactions of the other person or people involved tend to cause me the greatest worry and anxiety. 'What if' questions bubble up rapidly from below my conscious mind. We all have our little particular fear or weak point and learning to deal with it and being open to the way the universe assists us in overcoming it is vital. We simply cannot do it alone. Some tasks really can seem very daunting and overwhelming. Emotional decisions are especially hard to make because the heart and mind are in conflict.

The battle that rages inside needs one moment of calm so that we can hear the solution. This is why solitude is such a gift. Although we all need people, I really believe that we all need time to ourselves as well. Even with the best people around us decisions of the heart need to be made by one person alone: us. No one else can really know for sure what the best answer is.

Being creative, doing our art and experiencing the bliss of solitude are all helpful here. Sometimes things just need to take time. Moral courage develops with facing our difficulties and overcoming them. No one enjoys pain or suffering but we simply cannot avoid having them come into our life from time to time. Fortunately, we can grow stronger and be more adept at how we handle them. This is very encouraging.

Jung, who spent a lifetime helping people, observed

that our difficulties are necessary for health. Perhaps I can conclude this chapter by saying that the difficulties that I've had have led me to seek health and well-being and make it one of my top priorities. Maybe the experiences you are having now also call for this kind of attention. We are always striving for a better quality of life and a greater wholeness. Artists especially benefit from the gift of solitude to achieve this aim. Sometimes in order to create something new we must be willing to destroy something old. We just have to be brave. Solitude can make us strong.

CHAPTER 9

FOCUS – FINDING THE GIFT IN OUR IMAGINATION

I learned so much from reading Jung's work as well as those of his followers. They opened my mind to the fascinating and rich world within and often validated my thoughts, feelings and experiences in a completely unique way. In short, I began to trust myself more and more. I also began to value my imagination and to develop a tender faith that it would lead me into a brighter life. Such is the power of a lifetime's work like Jung's.

Many of us yearn for a fuller life that is rich with meaning and love. When we are creating like we do as artists, we are bringing the love inside us into physical form.

There are all kinds of love but for me, love is a powerful feeling full of warmth and tenderness. I won't say that I feel exactly this when I paint but I do feel a strong sense of joy and enthusiasm as I create my paintings. Imagination is like a butterfly that rests gently on my shoulders and encourages me to look beyond what I see in front of me to its hidden essence and inner qualities.

It is a close friend of intuition. Both imagination and intuition come into play when I paint. Imagination enables me to see the vision of the work and intuition allows me to work from my heart. With love and passion. The play of imagination, as Jung suggests, is valuable because it is whimsical and gentle in the way it unfolds mysteries for us. It is not easy to articulate all of our feelings and experiences in words, so imagination takes us into different and often higher realms. Flights of fancy are common, and they make art worth the challenge she presents.

IMAGINATION AND ART

Art is the embodiment of imagination. Not all of us can paint or draw but all of us can apply ourselves to be artistic and do things in an artful way. There is an art to everything that life offers us. An art to listening, an art to raising children, an art to better relationships and art to valuing who we are. All this implies being or becoming imaginative. When something does not work out for us in the way that we would like it to we can call on imagination to help us out. We can face the unknown by imagining what we would like instead of what we have today.

Some people say that they do not have dreams. What they are really saying is that their imagination has gone quiet. Of course, it is still there, and it just needs to be invited. We can do this by learning to be still, by being quiet and by listening to our hearts. Our hearts are full of wisdom and knowing and can help us out in our most desperate moments. The eye of imagination is a heartbeat away when we are conscious that we need some help. There really is no need to be in a state of despair for very long. Instead of despairing about our situation, we can turn to the universal source of faith and grow wings of hope.

We can read inspiring books, we can visit art galleries, we can go to see a dance performance, we can listen to music; really we can tune into other people's creativity and allow ourselves to be moved and to be inspired. Even doing something simple like baking some fresh bread or delicious muffins can cheer us up. Joy and happiness are imagination's allies. Watching movies can sometimes be very helpful in clearing out our emotions. When our mood is low, we can take some action; any action to lift ourselves out it and turn towards life.

EMOTIONS

Our emotions can be fuel for our imaginations. Feelings come in all the colours of the rainbow and each might require a unique action from us. If we are feeling good, we can continue to feed that feeling by doing more of what we enjoy and share it with others. This can be done through a conversation or a creative work of some kind. If we are feeling frustrated, we can journal about the subject. Anger and fear can be expressed in metaphors through a poem. Even reading other people's poems can stir our imaginations.

Pause for a while and consider all the moments in your life when you have felt especially inspired. What did your imagination lead you to do and to accomplish? How did you feel as a result of that achievement? What can you do now to break out of a situation that is no longer serving your best interest? Asking oneself questions such as these, or making up your own, will also kick start your imagination. We are all different in what makes our hearts sing so we will all feel inspired by different things.

Having said this, I think that the wonders of nature cannot fail to move anybody. The creativity inherent in nature is the master teacher. Everything is designed beautifully and perfectly. From the smallest flower to the great bright sun, all of nature's creations are there not only for our pleasure and to enhance our well-being but to teach us to see.

NATURE

Nature is real. It does not pretend, and it does not offer fakes. There are no fake trees or fake flowers or fake spiders. It exists as it is. She is a master professor in enabling us to see ourselves as we are; to drop our pretences and to just be. When we let ourselves be and accept that, like nature, we are designed beautifully, we can begin to grow towards the light and towards a sense of wholeness. It is only in thinking that there is something wrong with us that we feel stunted in our growth. When we become more self-assured and accepting of all our qualities we can begin to shine.

Imagination can play a great part in this. Think about the imagination of little children. They make up their own games and imaginative play is one of the best ways for them to learn. If they are allowed to use their imaginations, their play is intrinsically joyful and beneficial for them. We all love play. Even adults, who do things in a way that is filled with fun for them, blossom in a way unique and true to their own nature. Art allows for this. But so does any profession that is freely chosen and carried out with a heart. Feeling good in one's work is the best canvas for imagination to have free rein upon.

We don't need to be afraid of where imagination will take us if we become open to it. It is a guide that does not betray. Things might not always come easy but partnering with imagination we can face our difficulties with more ease. How often do we need to solve problems that can seem daunting and overwhelming to us? It can be a big relief to know that we don't have to do it alone. When we have faith and a sense of trust in the overall harmony and order of the universe we can let go of our struggles and take things one day at a time.

Some things cannot be solved quickly and the solution takes time to unfold. We can learn from the lives of flowers in this matter. They don't flower first. They start off as seeds then grow to become buds. Each stage of their blossoming is done gently. There is no force or effort there, just a slow and steady becoming.

This is the same with us. Some of us bloom earlier than others, but since I don't really believe that life is a competition we can each take our own time. What does it matter if Joe next door is ahead of us in something that we also desire when we are unique as individuals? It makes no difference if someone is more or less successful than we are because we are all learning all the time.

In addition, our ideas of success may differ from someone else's. Maybe you might like to pause and consider what success means for you and imagine yourself as being that success. And then continue to work towards that image of you until you become that person. We all have a right to be successful and I would add that we have a need to be successful on our own terms.

MOVING TOWARDS SUCCESS

Imagination can guide us. If we are feeling stuck for ideas, we can look outside for images that resonate within us. We can pick a picture that best symbolizes, for us, our own definition of success and put it where we can see it every day for it to remind us. In the meantime, we can appreciate where we are and all that we have achieved so far.

We are all working on ourselves all the time. This

is normal; this is natural. This is required of us. This does not mean that we criticise ourselves to achieve our aims because this doesn't really work. Imagine yourself as a little child who needs your affection and encouragement.

So how does imagination help us with our identity? Well, both words start off with the lovely little letter: 'I.' You are at the centre of your identity as well as your imagination. Think of yourself as an expression of God just as all of creation is an expression of God. I am not saying that we are God – this is not true – but we are his creation with the added bonus of having free will. This is good news because as his creation we can be confident that we are gifted with creativity, and our free will allows us to use it. It is a joy to use our creativity.

How we use it is up to us but ideally it would mean that we are enjoying what we are doing, and we are becoming more and more happy. This does not mean that we are happy all the time – that would be unnatural – but overall and inside we feel confident that we can create this positive state with more ease and more often. Yes, such wonders do happen when we use our imagination and create things that please us.

We can also develop a sense of trust, that what is genuinely pleasing to us will be pleasing to some other people as well. Maybe we will not please everyone but that would be highly unusual and completely unlikely. So, giving up that notion can set us even more free to do 'our thing' and be content with that. That is enough. Some people will tell us that we can achieve anything. I am of the mind that we can achieve what is in us to achieve, according to our own gifts, means and imagination.

KEEPING HAPPINESS ALIVE

I love the imagination that I have for painting my own pictures of flowers. I feel honest, bone-deep satisfaction when I paint and that is good enough for me. I can paint and this makes me happy. I am grateful for having this gift and I wouldn't swap it for any other because this make me, 'me.' I love being an artist. It is a great way to appreciate beauty in all its manifestation.

I value the work of other artists and feel privileged to be a part of this group of people who work with their hands. Working with my hands has always been a source of pleasure ever since I was a little girl. I have loved colour all my life. It just took a little while and a big detour to identify that painting is my profession. But I made it to this recognition and so can you if this is what is in your heart to do. Just begin. Any moment in time is good so let this be your moment.

If you are feeling unsure just use your imagination for now and imagine yourself as an artist. What mental picture do you get? If it is a positive one, then I would encourage you to go ahead and make a start. Perhaps you are a beginner and you feel that you need to take some lessons. Maybe you are intermediate or advanced and you want to progress in unconventional ways. Whatever seems best why not give it a go? If being an artist is who you are, this is it. You don't need to look elsewhere or envy others who are 'making it' in other professions. Decide that you will make it as an artist. We can all make this decision and then take the necessary steps to achieve our aims.

It might be true that in a conventional world being an artist is unconventional but so be it! We can only be who we are. Regardless of what 'people' might think or say, this is the life we have and we can do with it what pleases us, especially when what we are doing reflects our heart's true desires.

Why be something or someone we are not? Our imagination won't let us be dishonest with ourselves for very long. We will be guided to do things that will leave us pleasantly surprised. How about that life drawing class? And so on. Little by little we start to water the artist in our hearts and we become protective of her growth. We will no longer stand by and live lives that don't reflect our values of beauty, harmony and love.

OUR UNIQUENESS

We will be like nature – free, wild and true. We will become more enchanted with our own unique design and the designs of our work. As we create we will grow in self-appreciation. If you have come from a background that doesn't value art or artists I think it is helpful to go to exhibitions and galleries to observe just how many people there are who love art. Society as a whole does not reflect 'art lovers.' Art lovers are ordinary men and women who are moved by beauty.

Having faith when we begin will mean having faith as we continue and journey to our own promised land. Our imagination will keep showing us the way step by step with each of our pictures reflecting back to us what matters to us and what we want. What we see in our work and acknowledge is what we will value and have more of. I love flowers and I find that wherever I look I notice them. Whenever I notice them I feel better. Their beauty is always captivating and reminds me of the sense of wonder that I used to feel for everything as a child.

I was once walking home from my studio carrying a red amaryllis. Coming towards me was a mother pushing her little boy (about three years old) in a buggy. As they came closer the boy leaned forwards and looking at my flower exclaimed, 'Oh, my God!' I let him touch the flower since I know that little children like to touch everything, and his smile was beautiful to behold. An amaryllis made a little child happy! This gave me so much pleasure, to share beauty and to hear his sense of awe and appreciation.

BEING OPEN TO LIFE

No two flowers are the same, even if they are in the same flower family. To me this shows the endless variety of imagination. We can all feel encouraged by this as this shows that we need never feel that we are out of ideas. The world constantly feeds us with ideas and inspiration, we just need to be able to stop and observe.

Becoming observant, learning to see and hear things, as well as being open to the new, will always help us. Images are everywhere. We just need to trust that we have a unique sense of what images speak to us personally and then to have the confidence to make our art from these images. In my home now, I have some white lilies in a clear vase. They give such a presence of grace and elegance to my simple home that I often look at them to get a feeling of calm. This state of calm is the best one for flights of fancy.

Without imagination our lives can feel colourless. With it our lives can take on colour and we benefit in a myriad of ways. Don't let anyone tell you that you have no imagination. You do, and it is your golden path to a better life. So please learn to dance with it, learn to love who you are and live the life that enriches you! It is yours for the taking. It is time to be the real you; the one who is full of the imagination that rocks this planet (or your own world)!

CHAPTER 10

LOVE

I am the light of the world – Jesus

Our imagination can sometimes be a helpful agent towards developing our faith. Who and what we have faith in is unique for each of us. This chapter takes a look at love personified in Jesus. Everyone will have their own idea of who Jesus is, but if you are a Christian you will know and believe in your heart that Jesus is God. This knowledge keeps your life active and safe at the same time.

It doesn't mean that we will not experience difficulties, but it does mean that we have someone so special and unique to talk about it with and get guidance from. Without light we live in darkness. Darkness can be our fears, our limiting beliefs, general anxiety and maybe at times a sense of hopelessness or despair. Coming out from darkness into the light is a journey, just like it was for the Jews coming out of Egypt and being led to the promised land by Moses.

We may be at a point in our life when we have felt a restlessness or maybe we've even felt stuck in a situation that we feel has been holding us back. We want change, but we also resist change. The familiar may be stifling but the new is uncharted territory. So, what can we do? Well, we can ask for guidance. If we go to the source of this guidance we can turn our eyes and hearts towards God. We can also help ourselves by looking for guidance from other qualified and trustworthy people. We need not feel that we have to do it on our own. Even as I write this I smile because I love to do things on my own and I often think I can manage things just fine if I take care of it myself.

I will happily ask for help when I need it but mostly I like to work on my own. As an artist, this has both benefits and drawbacks. To paint I don't need another person, but to bring my art to the awareness of other people, as all artists know, I need others to help me. We need to interact with each other and begin to be part of this beautiful world that we live in. I say it is a beautiful world because I have felt the presence of a guiding force for a very long time, so I feel confident that I am always supported in one way or another. It wasn't always this way for me and perhaps not for you either. Having faith is one of the bravest decisions we can make for ourselves. It can turn our life around.

FAITH

Faith works in mysterious ways, uniquely for each one of us. The things that help me keep my faith may be different to what helps you maintain yours. However, underneath it all is the basic need and desire in all of us to feel safe and protected. Inner guidance is available all the time to help us with this. We cannot grow and make any kind of progress if we do not feel safe on a fundamental level. Once this is in place then we are more open to taking necessary risks.

If we feel for some reason that we do not have this faith, we can ask for it. It is never too late, and it is not a sign of weakness. To rely on a strong God is to admit that we need His love and help. If I look back over the course of my relatively short life I can see that I have always had the support I needed to keep going. Even at the most painful moments, there was some kind of saving grace. It was only ever very difficult when I suspended my belief and gave in to doubts and fears. Luckily, I have enough resilience to bounce back and I am sure that you do too.

The light that we seek is also seeking us. We need the light because we are people of the light and the light needs us because we are His. Jesus does not give up on us, even in moments when we may have given up on ourselves. His hand is always reaching out to us and His ears are ready to listen when we call out to Him. The book of psalms is rich with the heartfelt words of the psalmist to his God. When we bring our innermost thoughts and open up our feelings to God, He is gracious and giving towards us. He never betrays us, He is our friend.

His word lives in our hearts as guidance from within. We can rely on His word to navigate the waters of our life. By reading the Bible, we can become familiar with Him and in praying we can relate to Him exactly for who he is: a very real presence and a true person.

We can allow Him to show us how to become the person we were born to be. I am not sure who else can really do this better, since He knows us best. Naturally, we learn about ourselves in healthy relationships with other people, but for a true mirror I would still go to Jesus. His love is deep and wide, and He has space in His heart especially for those who love him sincerely.

ACCEPTING OURSELVES

We can read many books that tell us that we are 'divine.' This can be very pleasant news and we can each take it as we will, but I feel that we are also meant to be human and accept being human with gratitude. Being human means that we make mistakes and we can learn from them. Our humanity gives us compassion towards our fellow human beings going through life the best way they know how, also making mistakes, sometimes stumbling and we can help them out when called to do so.

Jesus is both human and divine. He is a person and He is also spirit. We can worship Him, and we can relate to Him. Actually, if we are going to worship anybody it is advisable that we worship the one who is worthy and who will honour our feelings of love and affection. When we worship mortals like ourselves, we can become disillusioned at some point, sometimes in very distressing ways. Why put our trust completely in people who are fallible like us when we can put it in someone who is truly trustworthy and will not let us down. When we know Him, and we believe in Him we can progress on our journey with greater joy and a sense of purpose.

Even thinking about Jesus can light up our thoughts and feelings because His character is excellent. If we have had difficult relationships in our lives, we may take some time to warm to the idea that Jesus is different, and we can relate to Him in ways that are healthy.

As artists, when we are in touch with this light we are in touch with something sustaining in ourselves. We have a fountain of resources available to us that we can rely on to keep doing our work. Michelangelo's masterpieces are a testament to the strong faith he had in a God he was convinced of. How else could he have developed his talent and mastered such diverse yet related branches of creative expression and knowledge? His divine and innate gifts grew, I believe, with his faith. He created because he believed, and he believed because he trusted this light.

When I read Vasari's *The Lives of the Artists* I was also struck by the fact that Georgio Vasari was clearly a man in full possession of his sanity and clarity. He knew who he was, like so many of the artists whom he portrayed so vividly in his book. Perhaps this shows us that artists really are meant to know who they are; to have faith in what they do and to bring more of God's light to the world. Although I said that ours is a beautiful world, we all know that there is also much pain, sadness and suffering. Maybe not all men hunger for this light but those of us who do can grow our faith, develop our talent and serve the God who created us.

APPRECIATION

Whether you are a believer or not, it does not harm you to consider the awesome design of the natural world. It does not show random chaos but rather intricate attention to detail. They say the devil is in the detail, but I say that God's handiwork *is* the detail. When we stop to appreciate the scent of the rose we can marvel at its form and colour and we can pause to consider that something that grew out of the Earth smells like heaven. Maybe nature is teaching us every day to become believers.

What we believe is for us. Your beliefs are yours and if they make you happy and give you answers to the questions that bother and concern you then that is good. Who knows? Maybe one day the light will beckon you. This glowing light is so gentle in its call that perhaps when you keep an open mind you will be open to its soft, tender voice and you will follow where it leads you.

For some reason – I am not sure why – many of us are very curious about our identity and our purpose here on Earth. As people we are protective of our uniqueness and our individuality. If you have ever experienced identity theft you may know how violating it feels. Many of us also care very much about our fellow human beings and our planet and we want to be part of making things whole, just as we want to be whole. Wholeness is so desirable that we will go to great lengths to accomplish this goal. We like the pieces of the puzzle to fit. If one is missing we go in search of it and will not rest until we have found it.

Jesus can become our strength. The joy of loving someone so good is a very powerful antidote to any sadness we may feel. With him as our source of strength, we can feel renewed each day and continue with our story. How do you take to the idea of your life being part of God's story? When we enter into a relationship with Jesus, we don't really realise that our lives matter. We may feel so small and insignificant that we have difficulty that someone as great as Jesus believes in us and is ready to assist us in believing in ourselves.

God is a great storyteller. He understands plot, character, intrigue and – above all – He has a gift for making the most complex situations simple enough to understand. They may take several readings but each time we are given a glimmer of understanding that inspires our faith. His people are people, just like you and I, so we can be secure in the knowledge that even if we don't have a sense of belonging with certain people in our lives, we belong with God.

BEING REAL

We don't have to be perfect – Jesus loves the real people. People have gone to Him looking for love, for health, for healing, for teaching, for food and He gave generously. His best friends were fishermen and simple women. I have always appreciated how much Jesus valued women because for some reason there are some upside-down ideas and attitudes to women prevalent in our world that are completely out of touch with Jesus's view. Above all, to Jesus, women and men are equal. There is no difference in the value of each to God. Why some men and women have got different ideas is a reflection of a world-view that is out of sync with truth.

Light is truth. Those who come to the light start to get clearer ideas of how things really are in the eyes of the one who matters, not to those who do not. The latter are people who continue to act in ways that are harmful to the human spirit. When women are subjugated, men also give up a part of their humanity. When women are seen as equal, men also benefit in exactly equal measure. And vice versa. There are far more known and famous male artists then women, but this need not be an issue at all for female artists working today.

Much has changed in the world and today women, like men, have equal opportunities for art education. We are not restricted to making things to satisfy the needs of patrons, we can follow our own hearts and create works of art that best reflect our love and our individual creativity. This is such a great gift and we can treasure this.

So, whether we love to paint animals, nature, people or things from our imagination, we are not restricted. We can, however, become agents of this loving light and seek to improve whatever it is we love doing continuously and for the benefit of both ourselves and other people.

If we need a counsellor God's spirit is always on hand. His angels (messengers) are ever with us. I am not an expert on angels, but I have benefited from the work of people like Doreen Virtue who are. It gives me comfort to know that angels look after me and help me out when I feel stuck. Knowing that they serve God and His people is reassuring. Getting positive messages from good books or Angel cards can be beneficial, as well as just fun. In short, I am a believer in the work of the angels and I am convinced that I am here and doing what I get to do because of their love and support.

The light is powerful. It can drive out darkness in a heartbeat. In my experience, (at least with me) God works slowly. Sometimes I feel that I am a slow learner in affairs of the heart and that my emotions take their time to heal, but I am now more accepting of this. As long as I get to where I want to be I am happy. I hope by now you are fairly aware that the light of love is very present in your heart as well.

Without following our heart's desires, both in our profession as creative people and in love, we may never come to claim the identity that is rightfully ours.

Our identity, however, does not let us go so easily. Who we are will keep knocking on our door until we open it. We were never meant to be alone. The light of the world will reveal to us our true colours and the image that we receive back will be the true one. Jesus means what He says. We just need to listen and to trust Him. We are made to love and be loved for exactly who we already are.

CHAPTER 11

RESPECT

In honour of the painter Masaccio, Annibale Caro wrote these words:

I painted and my painting was equal to truth;
I gave my figures poses, animation, motion,
And emotion. Buonarroti taught all others
And learned from me alone

– The Lives of the Artists

In his excellent book *The Lives of the Artists*, Vasari writes in a very moving way about the artists of the Renaissance. One of the best features of his writing is his strong praise for the artists and their accomplishments. The biographical sketches are lively, engaging and often full of rapture and passion for the various artists. He refers to Michelangelo as 'the most divine Michelangelo' and to Masaccio as the 'most excellent Masaccio.' It is a joy to read. Why? Because praise for excellence is so elevating and inspiring. It shows respect.

Praise is one of the highest gifts we can bestow on our fellow human beings when it comes from a sincere and loving heart. It does us a lot of good to be full of admiration for the efforts and achievement of people we admire, of those artists who have gone before us and created such wonderful works of art.

Reading *The Lives of the Artists* has been one of the best reading experiences of my life. It is like walking through the best art gallery with one of the liveliest minds in art history, who is Vasari himself. He is as likeable as many of the artists whom he praises. When we praise we are acknowledging the value of another human's achievement. It is the best heart surgery: it is completely benign and its effect on the heart is excellent. There are no side effects, in fact like Vasari does so brilliantly and seemingly effortlessly, the loving and positive current carries us away and we are made to feel that we too know such outstanding men and women.

Because his book is so lively it feels completely timeless. It can make the Renaissance seem like it was yesterday. The men he writes about created with a passion that exists within us all, maybe to different degrees but passion is passion!

HONOURING OTHERS

Honouring others helps us to honour ourselves. In this state of mind there is no need for envy because admiration is the best cure for this emotion. We all have it in us to envy others who are talented and achieving what we would like to achieve, but if we are honest we know that this is not necessary and is counterproductive. We can all create according to the measure of talent we have, and we can all shine. The evening sky is full of millions of stars and there is room for all of us here on Earth.

Creating cures feelings of inadequacy and envy. When we get busy 'doing our thing' we are happy, and happy people are not jealous of others. No one does things quite like us, so we can feel carefree in our own mode of expression. Expressing with beauty and excellence what is within us is all that is required. We are also in it for the long haul (think eternity) so there is no pressure. We can develop our skills and vision in our own time in a manner suited to us.

The Lives of the Artists is sacred text for all artists. The language is excellent, Vasari's mind is brilliant, and his humanity is deep and good. He is a sure guide to the artists he knew personally and his research on their work is thorough. He understands the people he wrote about and he respects their achievements. He understood that he lived among giants of art who were often exceptional people. I once read in an art magazine that great art comes from great artists. I really loved this! This feels especially true when reading 'Lives.' These artists were great people. They studied and practised their craft with complete devotion and laboured with great love over their masterpieces.

Sometimes we read something, or we see a great work of art, and something in us is released to reach for heights we did not see at the beginning of our journey. We may be ordinary people, living quiet lives and going about our business, but we can learn to see the beauty in our lives and create from the heart of this beauty. We get to be alive and we get to be creative! How wonderful is that!

HONOURING OURSELVES

Even if there is not a lovely Vasari among our midst to celebrate our work (however great or modest), we can praise, respect, honour and appreciate what we do. We can do this most effectively not when we compare ourselves to others but when we look back at where we have come from. This awareness of our own course is the best recipe for self-confidence that I have found.

Self-confidence is about us. Not about others. We can read the lives of the great artists and learn much from them – perhaps just even feel good that we are among other artists – but we need to get clear about our own good self. If we have ignored this creative self for a long time, we can now choose to focus on her and raise her so that she too can grow towards the sunshine. We have all heard the saying that whatever we focus on grows. When we keep our eye on other people we may be neglecting what we need to pay attention to in our own life. We need to take care of our own self and grow as artists and as individuals. The two can go together. Self-care becomes at first more complex, then more simple.

It takes a lot of effort at first to become aware of habits that we need to change in order to become more like our real nature intends us to be. If we need to learn something it takes time, effort, investment and energy. This is the complex part. Once we have learned something it becomes simpler, as it becomes a natural way in which we operate and express ourselves in the world.

The value of our art is something for us to decide. Maybe at first, we feel insecure about pricing our art. Who can measure the love, the knowledge, the labour and all the other elements that went into making our art? As we come to value the core of who we are, we get more comfortable with the prices that we set. Finding customers for our work is also an art. We would like people who value our art as much as we do and are happy to live with it. People have different ideas of what art is, but for me a work of art is one that appeals to the sensibility of beauty and makes someone feel good.

The 'Lives' shows us the artists whose work has endured over time. Their work is ever loved because they show skill, talent and vision. The best artists mastered their craft and went beyond what existed before they came on the scene and created something truly original. There is really no need to copy what someone else is doing when you are being you!

YOUR OWN SONG

Bring forth what makes your heart sing and let your song go out into the world to enchant the people who are drawn to your work in particular. Understand these people and honour them. Show them kindness and value their feelings. There are many good people who value and appreciate art and there will be enough who will praise yours and be inspired by it. These people deserve our loyalty. As we know, no one's art is for everybody.

I once went to a talk on art at a church and the priest (!) said that he didn't consider Michelangelo a good artist. So, there it is. Even the best of the best have people who don't see the beauty in their art. This is sad, and we can say this priest is losing out on one of life's most extraordinary talents ever, but it makes the point that we need to be mindful of the special people who love our art. They are gems.

I have found my greatest sense of belonging among artists in the galleries that I have visited. The art that speaks to me best is the artist who I am drawn to. There are several and I have many favourites. This isn't a substitute for fellow artists and if we can find like-minded ones we are indeed blessed. Until we do, reading about great ones or getting to 'know them' by looking at their art, we are still in good company.

As artists we are, at heart, into making changes. I know I talked about how I can resist change in my life, but as an artist I am into change. I like to freshen up my colours, work magic on my canvas and get new inspiration all the time. Maybe if I (or you, if this is also true for you) can apply this childlike attitude to my life I might have an easier time with change. We can invite change just like we invite new experiences and become better adapted to the challenges that come with them.

The Renaissance period, as we know, was a time of re-birth in the arts and culture. Re-birth is such a beautiful word. It is used in Christianity to refer to a person whose heart has been converted to faith and in the arts, it means a re-birth of the appreciation for the beauty and excellence of antiquity. This is how I understand it. Maybe an expert in these fields has a different take on it.

BEAUTY

Throughout time, people have appreciated and valued the quality of beauty and perfection. There is something so truly inspiring about beauty that it is hard to put into words. It really has to be seen, felt and experienced. Really at its heart beauty is an agent of the divine. God has to be beautiful inside out to be worshipped so affectionately.

At its best, beautiful art executed with excellence touches the soul and puts one's spirit in touch with the divine that is within. This is not some fanciful idea but rather a truth that those who experience beautiful art feel. It may take some training, but really to my mind it is an exposure to excellent art. One does not get this exposure by looking at empty meaningless art, but by going to the world's best galleries or in the absence of this opportunity looking at great works of art in libraries or book stores.

This may seem like some effort, but the effort is well rewarded. It becomes a pleasure to gaze at a work of art that speaks to one and touches the 'beauty spot' within one's soul. Then one can develop a language of feeling for particular art and become more comfortable with beauty itself. This has been the desire of the best artists. They sought to keep finding new ways of describing their version of the beautiful and to practice their devotion to something beyond themselves.

The 'Lives' is a great mirror to all artists. We all need praise and encouragement, and even reading such lofty words for other artists puts one in a good and inspired mood. We see what we might become if we keep up with our practice and follow faithfully the course of our own nature.

It has been said that we read to know that we are not alone, and I would like to imagine that Georgio Vasari wrote this book to help other artists who would come to know this. He observed first hand the difficulties some artists faced, and he wanted to be of comfort to future artists. I am convinced of this. At the end of his book, he has a special chapter dedicated to 'Artists of the Art of Design,' and he writes this: 'Most honourable and noble artisans, mainly for whose sake and benefit I undertook such a lengthy task a second time...' So, you see! We are so loved that someone great had us in mind even before we arrived to take up the work. The art of design is a beautiful subject and we who do it are among the fortunate.

I have to be honest here, it took me a long time to think of being an artist in this way. But I am coming around and the 'Lives' was a major turning point for me. So as far as I am concerned, Mr Vasari has touched my life significantly. I hope that if you haven't read this excellent book, by such a venerable writer, that you would consider doing so. This is especially true if you are struggling to accept who you are and what you are here to do.

TUNING IN

We are here to love, to create, to paint and to live as free citizens devoted to our loving God. It is so very simple only sometimes we make it complicated, whether it's because of the fears we harbour, the insecurities we feel or the difficulties we have had. But help is on hand. Join in. Tune in to the wonders of nature if you have no one else to share your life with at the moment. Nature is an artist's best friend.

An artist can feel at home in nature because nature teaches her what is natural. The concrete and the city jungle are all full of inspiration too – especially in cosmopolitan cities because there is so much to see – but as we know because of our sensitivity it is also stressful. Nature relaxes us and reveals the flow and pattern of the natural world.

When we admire a little duckling or watch a heron in flight, we can immerse our senses to the awesome delight of being alive. And then we can increase our praise for the glory of nature and the great creator behind it all. As we study, work and observe, we grow a better understanding of who we are. Perhaps the answers we seek won't come served on a plate, but we can have more fun with life and be open to things we never considered possible when we were living with fear and anxiety.

Really, in this chapter I wanted to encourage all of us to take heart. If we are feeling out of sorts, it is best to take some time out. If we don't know what to do next, we need some peace and relaxation. We can then allow the answers to come slowly and we can take action on the one that seems the best. I talked about the value of praise, appreciation and respect for ourselves, other people and life itself. It is an attitude of reverence for all that we are, all that we have, and all that we are becoming.

The 'Lives' is full of these sparkling qualities that make the heart sing and the mind take leaps of imagination. We come to know that what we honour is a reflection of who we are. This can give us great courage, wisdom and quiet strength. When we let great authors like Vasari be one of our guides in the world of art and artists, we enhance not only what we know but we also get a sense of what and who 'knows' us. This is a great honour.

CHAPTER 12

DEDICATION

Men of genius sometimes accomplish most when they work the least, for they are thinking out inventions and forming in their minds the perfect idea that they subsequently express with their hands – Georgio Vasari, *The Lives of the Artists*

Creativity, in my experience, often calls for short burst of inspired activity followed by spells of doing 'nothing.' Sometimes people ask me how long I take to do a work of art, and when I tell them that it takes just a few hours or half a day I can tell that they are somewhat surprised. This is also partly because of my temperament. I like to be efficient and I like to work quickly. I can perceive in my mind's eye what I want the finished work to look like, and I gradually work towards creating that image. I just know where to place things on the canvas and I enjoy working intuitively with colour. This all comes with practice and every artist approaches her work differently.

But I would agree with Vasari's quote. It may take some time to collect all the items to create the overall effect, but once inspired the painting 'time' doesn't necessarily need to take that long. There are many artists like Vermeer who painted very slowly and over a long period of time, but clearly his vision was very different from someone like Van Gogh who painted with passion and a different vision.

Taking time off from doing creative work is very healthy. We are human beings first and we need to recharge. Time out is part of the creative process. The impact of creating can often be strong on our senses and make demands on our abilities and we all have other needs besides being creative all the time.

Rest is often best. It is soothing to the creative spirit to engage in doing nothing and just enjoying some peace and quiet. In this state, we can allow our minds to wander and dream up all kinds of things pleasing to our souls. We can fantasise, we can plan, and we can feel the freedom of just being alive.

Leisure is not a luxury but a necessity for those of us who are committed to having a creative life and bringing our colourful visions into the world. It may initially feel unusual or even selfish to do something for ourselves, but it pays good credit to our human self. We know that we are productive when the time calls for it, so we can rest in good faith when we need to. Going somewhere pleasant like a park and watching the ducks floating on the pond can reinvigorate us and fill us up with love of life.

DISTRACTIONS

The wisdom of doing something else is rich with possibilities. When we are doing other things, we are allowing our creative tanks to be replenished. Sleep is a great restorative. Making sure that we get enough sleep is vital for artists (and for everyone really, as we know). The beauty of sleep is that the dreams we have – whether we are aware of them or not – transport us out of the physical world into the spiritual world. As Jung said in his book *Dreams*, they protect sleep. Some artists have dreamt up their next painting in their dreams. Personally, I haven't, as I take my inspiration from real life and I need to physically see the flower that I want to paint, but again we are all unique in our approaches.

Also, ideas come best when we are receptive to them, as we mentioned earlier, and for that to happen we need to be in a gentle state of mind. Ideas are all around us. Once we have a better insight into who we are and what makes our creative hearts sing, we can better perceive these ideas and make them our own.

We might decide to go to the movies and find that one single frame of the movie gives us the idea for our next work of art. The same inspiration can come from a line of a song or a metaphor from a poem. If we are used to recording our thoughts and valuing how we experience our life as we are living it, then we can recognise the ideas that we wish to realise creatively.

Relaxation is key. What relaxes us often energises

us as well. How do you relax? What is your favourite way to unwind and distract yourself from your 'to do' list? Paying attention to what gives you joy and space in your mind is a very helpful practice. I find reading with a latte very relaxing and at the same time, I am aware that it recharges me. For me, reading is part of my everyday existence. It is a habit.

I also love to swim because I move my body in a way that offers a kind of meditation for my mind at the same time. When I am in water, I feel at home. It is as natural as going for a walk or painting for me. Of course, in the beginning it didn't offer these benefits instantly as I had to learn the strokes and I needed to focus on the detail of getting them right, but after years of practice I can now say that it is practically effortless.

For me, swimming is like therapy. I release all my thoughts into the water and the water relaxes and rejuvenates my mind. The positive overall effect is immeasurable! I once met a lovely lady in the locker room as we were changing, and we were talking about the benefits of swimming. She said that for her swimming in water feels like a spiritual experience every time. Sometimes I think of what she said and how the water transports her beyond the physical. Maybe you too have an activity that offers such benefits for your own body and mind.

MEMORIES

As I am typing this, I just received a post card from my mother in Spain. It is the picture of Picasso's *Harlequin*. I love this painting. A copy of this painting hung in my bedroom that I shared as a child with my sister in Hungary. It makes me think back to days that seemed long with simple toys to play with. I used to find the little boy in this painting a little sad, but the artfulness of the painting stayed with me.

So, what does this picture tell me (and us) about clues to my identity? If we reflect for a moment and look back to our childhoods, we will discover many things that we may be in the habit of overlooking. As children we are very curious.

If we absorb a lot of negative things our souls can become heavy inside us. Like the little harlequin boy, we can become a bit thoughtful and wise for our age. At the same time, there is always a flip side to everything. We might even discover that 'art' had its hand on us by the way of images such as these from a very young age.

I remember that my aunt's family, who lived next door to us, had the prints of Toulouse Lautrec on their wall. My creative little mind loved the funny looking dancers on the print. I was drawn to the world of art even from my childhood. And I suspect if you are an artist so were you.

Images called out to us and fascinated us. They made us wonder about things unknown to us, but which somehow felt 'close' to us. The little boy harlequin in this image was a child, just like I was: a little thoughtful, innocent and loved to dress up and make believe.

I have always loved the little blue and yellow diamond patterns on my little harlequin. These colours are so bold together and they speak to me of creative expression. Colours and their special use tell stories wonderfully. When we look at a painting by Van Gogh, we can tune in to his thought processes and especially to his feelings about what he was painting. Colours 'tell' us that he loved the yellow house and he felt strong joy for it against the blazing blue background. The heat that comes from the house transports us to Southern France and into Van Gogh's heart. He knew what he was seeing, and he felt what he painted. He was a master storyteller as a painter. Wouldn't you agree?

Perhaps if you consider your own favourite artists you can tell (maybe more intuitively) what stories they are bringing to life with their paintbrushes. We, as artists, love to describe and give a voice to what we love. Don't we all want to have our voices heard? Especially if we were often silenced as children, our voices can become like volcanos in our throats and fire from our brushes.

SILENCE VERSUS EXPRESSION

Maybe we like to paint because we hate being silenced. Art does not keep us quiet. It calls for expression and adventure with all that we wish to say. And if we have ever been silenced, we may well feel that actually we have a lot to say.

Children should be heard and seen. They have a big contribution to make to our understanding of life. Their honesty is refreshing, natural, often funny and very interesting. They are simply wonderful. Their love and joy is their natural state and when we encourage their natural state we become part of their world. Being part of a child's little world is exciting. They have much to share and their generosity needs to be acknowledged and respected. When I worked with children was when I felt most in touch with who I am on the inside. I did miss being creative, but I loved the joy I felt bubbling up inside me in their presence. Also, their spontaneous affection is an immense reward for anybody who is kind to them and treats them well.

I think that artists and children go very well together. Artists are typically in touch with the little child inside them and children are very creative. I learned things from children that no book has ever taught me. I learned to be more natural. I learned that I felt good around little children. They still brighten up my days whenever I think of them and I keep them in my heart. I often wonder what they are doing now. They have made deep grooves of love and gratitude in my mind and they have touched my heart.

As artists we are sensitive to colour and we respond to strong images. What we love will be special for us. Sometimes I just pick up random cards from stationery stores because they spark my imagination. At the start of writing this book, I bought a beautiful painting of a parrot by Becky Brown in Ryman's. The picture is just the head of the bird and a bit of its upper body and the colours are great: red, yellow, a speck of green and some blue. Its eyes are kind of shy, but alert. I felt that it went really well with the title of the book. This parrot has got such a strong sense of identity because of its form and bold colours.

MARKS OF IDENTITY

Identity has these qualities: a clear signal of who or what someone or something is. It is, to my mind, an inside job. We may collect information from the world around us but as artists we need to develop this strong sense of self. We may get it wrong until we get it right. Once we are comfortable with our qualities, it becomes easier to communicate who we are to the outside world.

Fortunately, we can do this. It may take a little time for some of us and the path isn't always easy, but guides are here to help and support us. We just need to trust our own instinct about how we make use of all the information. Eventually, we become aware that while our identity shifts and changes, there is something very distinctive about 'us.'

This is the joy of the journey. This is the quest, this is the gem we are searching for. This elusive and distinctive 'je ne sais quoi.' Like the bold parrot we are bold individuals, otherwise we would not bother. We would put our feet up and stare with glazed over eyes at the television. Not for us such tunnel vision. We are creatures of the natural world. Born free, wild and very much alive. Whatever obstacles we have overcome we did it and will continue to overcome.

Our distinctive quality or qualities are so masterfully and intricately put together that I believe it is only God who can reveal it to us. This divine spirit that lives in us wants to realise itself fully in us because we are His. Without Him (in my view) we don't exist as individual people. We may go on through life and be functional, but we do not become who we are meant to be.

How we build our relationship with the sacred and the divine is a matter for our own hearts. We are never alone, and we are always guided. Our free will can also assist us. If we have set our eyes on the prize – to have a clear sense of who we are – I believe that the entire universe will offer its support. Since not everyone is interested or engaged in this activity, we may not easily find this among everyday folk. So, we need to develop our vision for people who are 'like us.' People who are searching and who have similar values to us. They exist.

Look for people who move you. Who feel right. People who treat you with consideration and respect. Such people can serve you in your search for a deeper understanding and appreciation of who you are and you can have healthy relationships with them. Artists need great friends and loving support. Birds of a feather flock together.

My little parrot picture is a bold reminder to be myself. I value the thoughtfulness of the little harlequin, treasure his innocence and I love the self-expression that the parrot speaks of. A picture tells a story. A painting sometimes includes a lifetime's work of dedication. It is my hope that the dedication we feel for our art leaves us plenty of room for the rest and relaxation we need as human beings. To be fulfilled is the real work of art for all of us.

CHAPTER 13

HARMONY

In our own time it has been seen...that simple children roughly brought up in the wilderness, have begun to draw by themselves, impelled by their own natural genius, instructed solely by example of these beautiful paintings and sculptures of nature – Georgio Vasari, *The Lives of the Artists*

Here we have Vasari painting us a portrait of an artistic child inspired by the wonderful creation that is nature. We have already talked about how nature is the best teacher in so many ways. In her we find all the nuances of shape, colour and design, so it is only natural that the works inspired by her are the true great works of art.

When I was in high school, one of our English teachers had us write an essay on nature and her child: human nature. I have had to write numerous essays in school, but that is the only one I remember truly enjoying and learning from in the most intuitive way. It may come as no surprise that the essay was inspired by the book we were reading at the time: *The Adventures of Huckleberry Finn* by Mark Twain.

We, as artists, are all on an adventure. For some of us in this moment it is about finding the best course or teacher. For others, it is about finding our voice and our subject matter. Yet for others it is about figuring out a way to make a successful living from doing what we love. Whatever it is and wherever we are, when we follow the inspiration of nature we can be more confident that we will take the most natural route for ourselves and do things that feel in harmony with who we are and what we want.

When a child draws from nature that child begins to be able to describe a world that is beyond herself yet is also a part of herself. This positive dialogue has many wonderful benefits. That child grows up knowing herself. This is the ideal. When I was ten years old I had a drawing friend who I will call Eva. Eva and I would cycle to our favourite tree on our school's grounds (in Tokyo, Japan), climb it with our drawing pads and pencils, and copy cartoon images from Japanese Manga magazines.

Now this isn't drawing from nature, and perhaps we were missing out, but just sitting on the thick branch of the tree and drawing was a lot of fun for us. When I think back on it now, it feels like it was yesterday. Drawing is a very natural activity. Many children draw freely, and it is only as they begin school that the focus shifts to more left-brain types of knowledge. For me, this is a shame, because art is what comes from the heart. And really, it is our hearts that carry so much of

140

the wisdom that we need to lead lives of passion. It is also the seat of our courage.

RECONNECTING WITH NATURE

Nature provides an artist – young or old – with a sense of timelessness. It is never too late to begin as an artist. When I started to paint again I went to Regent's Park with the smallest canvas I could buy, my acrylic paints and I painted a single tree. It was one of the best artistic experiences I have had. I felt like a child again; open, trusting and learning. I marvelled at the colours I was seeing, and the personality of the little tree became more apparent to me as I painted her. This may seem far-fetched, but if you try it you might have the same experience. Drawing nature enhances our self-awareness in relation to her and this can only do us good.

Although being in nature is peaceful, nature is rarely silent. To enjoy silence in nature is a wonderful moment but nature, to me, is always speaking. The wind blows through the leaves, the birds are chirping, bees are buzzing and so on. Everything in nature has its own voice. When we draw from nature we are giving ourselves a voice about what we are perceiving. This is a unique gift that we can give ourselves. It is a way of finding our own self-expression. Nature helps us abundantly.

When we admire nature, we are growing inside us

in imperceptible ways. Remember that we talked about the benefits of admiring those who have gone before us, or those artists who are making beautiful art in the present times. This same approach towards nature is just as important. Nature is a mirror of our own human nature and vice versa.

We can become more accepting of ourselves when we witness similar nuances of 'behaviours' in nature. She is of many moods, like us. She can be gentle, she can be fierce, she can be wild, she can seem tamed, but really at heart nature is often unpredictable. This can help us accept that whilst nothing is certain, we can describe what is in front of us and this act alone is enough.

We have witnessed something, given it shape, form, colour and a voice. We become participants in our environment and not just people passing beauty by. Nature provides endless opportunities to become sensitive to beauty in a way that modern culture very often does not. Nature does not care if you are nine or ninety. Whatever your age you will find something in nature that reflects your beauty back to you.

Being in nature is the best medicine for a stressed state of mind. The green is very calming and cleanses our hearts. When we become agitated she offers us solace. There is a great ease in being in nature. Almost everything we need is provided for, as far as being happy and being more balanced. And it is free. Just think: all that wild beauty, all those trees, all that grass and all of its wild creatures for us to admire and appreciate. And if we feel so inclined: to draw and paint them.

When I was a child I loved climbing trees. Now I only climb one when I feel sad and I need to feel good again. Maybe I'd feel good all the time if I did more of what I did as a child! Climbing trees and colouring. It seems that now I need the comfort of my studio, but it's a thought.

Things in nature flourish and blossom. Of course, there are casualties, but for the purpose of this book and to inspire ourselves I want to focus on all the wonderful flowers that we can observe in their full blossom and all the trees – great and small – that flourish. This is how we are meant to be as well. Just like them we grow slowly and at our own pace, but the aim is still the same. To be who we are born to be.

ART AND LIFE

When we are not growing, we need to tune into our feelings and ask what is stopping us. It might be relationships, it might be our job, our health, whatever it is we can address it and take steps to remedy our situation. To get in the flow we need to let go. We can let go of the idea that we can control every outcome, but we need to take steps to influence what we can to make our lives healthier and better.

We need to have strong minds, strong hearts and healthy bodies. This is the ideal. As artists we are always working towards the ideal. If we don't have one of these then we tend to put our efforts into making these as good as they can be. None of us are perfect but we are all good enough exactly as we are, and our uniqueness is a testament to this fact.

In my mind, art and life are one. Art is at the service of life and life teaches art. We cannot learn about either from reading books. Like with everything else, we need to experience both. Art can be a way to experience life in a very special way. We engage with life in a gentle and appreciative way and we give back to life all the passion that we feel in being alive.

When we are being artistic we are embracing time. It is in those creative moments when time stands still and is at our command. I think if time were personified (and artists have done it) he would be very appreciative of all people who did what they loved to do.

This is how the universe makes progress. With everyone tuning into their own hearts and following the insights that their own heart gives them. Of course, we need to make some time for listening to our hearts. We cannot rush about and expect to hear what our hearts are whispering.

The next time you feel yourself being drawn to something, or to somebody, you can trust that it is your heart talking to you. This is only true if it feels good! An attraction should feel positive.

OUR PLACE IN THE WORLD

I have the idea that life was created so that man and God can work together to bring about a beautiful and healthy planet. Our job is to find out how we fit into this scheme and what our specific role is. We are either creators or we are healers. In some cases, we are both. Naturally, creativity exists in all kinds of work, not just in the specifically artistic endeavours. There are very creative lawyers and there are healing receptionists.

For those of us who believe in the great power of God, we may gradually grow in awareness that we are His children. This helps us let go of our fears and trust in the one we believe in to help us be whole and capable individuals. This is what we have been working towards throughout this book. Our need to be whole rests on our faith that we will be whole. We are not meant to come here and just exist. We are meant to claim who we are. Of course, this is a quest for many of us. It is a spiritual quest that we cannot deny, and we cannot ignore.

When we are honest with ourselves about what we want, we are far more likely to get it. This may mean that we start to open up our hearts and become more vulnerable. As long as we respect this, we can stay safe and open up only to those people who deserve to know how we feel.

There is freedom beyond the limitations we may presently be experiencing. As we believe this, wider frontiers open up in our minds. We begin to search for ways to grow and create. Our hunger for love and abundance becomes stronger. We want to leave behind the barren lands that we have travelled across and come to the oasis of inner peace and healthy, active living.

We become more grateful, and practising gratitude becomes second nature. This creates a positive upward cycle, as we find more and more things to be grateful for.

It is a good thing to see clearly and realistically and it is good to be appreciative of all that has gone well for us up to now.

We are always creating in the present moment. Keeping an open mind about how the universe works, how God works, how we work, helps us be more flexible about how we see ourselves. If we haven't always had a true and positive self-image, this begins to shift and change. Inside, we may always have known somewhere deep down that we are good artists and good people, but now we are becoming much more self-aware and this is for the best. This is how it should be.

DEEPER UNDERSTANDING

Self-awareness helps us to live life from a place of deeper understanding and compassion. This depth, versus the unconscious superficiality, is of vital importance. We begin to have a much broader idea of what it means for us to be alive and what we want from our lives. And we begin to feel this from the depths of our hearts. Once all this becomes more real, our mind chatter becomes less distracting.

We are living with a stronger sense of who we are and why we are here. We will meet many good teachers along the way who can guide us. Inside us – living in our hearts – is the best teacher of all. God's holy spirit gently guides us. He doesn't control us or take away our free will, but He knows what he is doing, and He knows whom He is dealing with. He knows *us*.

There is a cost to be who we are meant to be. I think subconsciously everyone knows this and this is why so many people are terrified to look deep within themselves. We know that we will have to give up certain things that we may have clung to for what we want.

These decisions are gut wrenching and, in my experience, do not happen overnight. It can take years. The word that comes to mind is *sacrifice*. We will need to sacrifice something that is a part of us to be free souls. This is not an easy matter. It may, in fact, be a moral matter. Whatever it is for you – for me – we need to be very brave. This is so easily said and so difficult to do. They say love is the strongest force in the universe, yet it also takes the greatest courage to love.

If we have been going at things solo and we are not happy with it, the sacrifice will entail giving up some cherished ideas about being single and some of the freedoms that we perceive it comes with. But there may be other things lurking in the background of the mind. Whatever it is, love is the answer. It is also the riddle.

Here, nature can help us. As we work through our dilemmas and come back to a sense of who we are when we are feeling good, we can take steps towards what we want. For some of us there are steps we take towards ourselves, for others it entails taking steps in the outside world. It can be both. I strongly believe that God and His angels are here to guide us and we are not left alone to take decisions that we feel are almost beyond us.

Nothing is impossible with God. The Bible teaches us this. All that seems impossible today is an invitation for God to step in and guide us towards our possibilities. Because He knows us, He works with us, and His guidance is trustworthy. We may need to take some actions that feel a little unusual at first, but all that is required is that we take the next step. So, I leave you with these two questions: Are you ready? And what is your next step? A small step faithfully taken is all that is required.

CHAPTER 14

SUCCESS – LIVING ON YOUR OWN TERMS

The Oxford English Dictionary gives a definition of success that is a good one: the achievement of an aim or a purpose. This definition is wonderfully flexible and can be very inclusive. We can use our imagination here. The best way to approach our definition of success in my mind is to consider where we have come from and where we are today. We, as human beings, are always dreaming of things we want to do and things we want to achieve. Some are modest aims whilst others are bigger ones. Becoming successful on our terms means that we listen to what is in our hearts. Let's consider some general aims that people might have:

To learn a new skill

To become financially independent

To sell their art

To lose some weight

To get fit

To be healthy

To develop discipline in a certain area

To be married

To travel the world

To own a home

And so on. Please add your own aim or wish list. If your definition of success is authentic to who you are, it is precious. We may admire other people who look successful, but really it is the fulfilment of our own heart's desires that is going to be meaningful to us. I think in our hearts we know this. People who are doing great things all the time inspire us, but we feel most inspiration when we are fired in our bellies by what we are doing. If we would love to bring beauty to the hearts of people through our art, then this is a genuine and worthy aim to have.

Whatever it is we want, when we make a commitment to it simply by writing it down we are more likely to be working towards it and getting it.

I love being an artist. When I am drawing or painting I feel most myself in my creative expression. Taking the next step to bringing my art to the world or my story to an audience feels like taking a bigger risk.

However, I remember when I started to paint again after a very long detour, that felt like a risk. I am just reading a book by Brene Brown called *The Gifts of*

Imperfection where she discusses the difficult emotions of shame, offers suggestions for shame resilience, and explores our vulnerabilities in putting ourselves 'out there,' telling our stories and being real. I find it hugely encouraging so if Brene ever reads this book – thanks!

Those of us who work from the heart often live from the heart. This is not always easy because it means that our feelings might get more easily hurt. Luckily, life moves us on and our feelings get repaired in another context.

Success with art is doing what we love, being who we are and finding our audience who loves what we do and appreciates it. This might take some time because we need space to create our work, perfect it and have something of value to offer. Being a perfectionist with our work is often inevitable for artists, but hopefully over time we loosen our perfectionism within ourselves.

The worth of our work is up to us and inevitably up to the people who wish to own one of our pieces. When we get the work right (that is we are true to our nature and what we are passionate about), the price right and we find our ideal customers, then the world can start spinning on its axis for us. Then somehow, however magically, we have found a bright solution for ourselves and for those who 'need' our art to liven up their lives, put a smile on their hearts and feel good.

STEPS TO SUCCESS

The steps to success are small. Our vision grows with our work and as we grow. When we start out with our first painting or our first drawing we are not necessarily thinking about an exhibition. We are just 'getting it' and practising. We are playing. As we continue with our labour of love, new dreams start to come in like ships on the horizon. Suddenly an exhibition seems like a good idea. Learning other skills becomes a necessity. We are always expanding our sense of self and releasing our potential.

Think about the person whom you consider to be the most successful. It might be someone famous, dead even, or someone very close to you. Consider what qualities of that individual make him or her successful in your eyes. And then ask yourself (honestly) whether you already possess those qualities. I would strongly imagine that you do. Otherwise it is not likely that you would admire that person. If you don't think those qualities in you have been realised or 'polished', well, you can always decide to do something about that.

The muscle of the heart is beautifully created. Your heart beats to your own passions just as my heart beats to mine. Our longings are there to inspire us and to move us to create the lives (and the success) that we want. The unique gifts that we have are not going to go away, but our hearts might feel sad if we don't express them. It takes courage to trust our hearts to show us how to live. This is not to dismiss our intellect, for we all need to be discerning, but the heart is the power engine of love. Without the love we have for our work, for each other, we do not feel fully alive.

If you have had a tough life so far and for whatever reason you have blocked your heart – take heart. You have not failed, you have not disqualified yourself from a successful life, you are simply in the process of learning to listen to your power engine. The driving force of your life that is your heart needs to be given some wings. As you engage in doing your work and reach out to people, your trust muscle is also growing. If we weren't afraid, we would all trust ourselves more. And this can be an aim!

A HEALTHY AIM

To aim is to drive home a message to the universe (kind of like aiming an arrow) that you want things to change for you and that you want things to work out for your highest good. This is important. We no longer want to sit on the sidelines admiring everyone else when our feathers are bright, and our own birthright is to shine as well and as much as anyone else.

We want a spiritual makeover. We want to be true to who we are, and we want to claim our birthright. You know the image you get back in the mirror when you decide to put on your favourite and most flattering clothes and your eyes are sparkling? That's the kind of makeover I am talking about here. Really, it starts from our hearts. It can take years of mental preparation, but one day your heart starts to shift. One day your heart is no longer numb, and she releases all of her pent-up feelings and blows your mind away with her presence.

The presence of your heart is something extraordinary. It has been 'there' all along, but suddenly you become so aware of her that you start to respect what she is telling you. Trust me, this is one of the most successful experiences one can have. This is especially true for those of us who have had difficult past experiences. What this means is that our hearts are ready to heal. We cannot heal what we are unwilling or unable to feel and acknowledge. It is not an easy experience to sit with strong emotions. That is why to feel certain feelings takes all of our courage.

But when we are fast becoming who we are and have always been, there is no more holding back. It is not a reversible process. We are engaging with the divine and He will not let us go if we trust in Him. The more willing we are, the more beautiful our spiritual makeover becomes. It is as I mentioned earlier, a conversion of our heart. We become more human. Somehow, we soften and become more full of compassion. We may have readily felt compassion for other people but now we also feel stronger compassion for ourselves. We begin to accept our humanity and our imperfections. In our uniqueness we are all special, and in our humanity, we are equal to everyone else.

BEING OPEN TO VIBRANT HEALTH

Some of the things that have plagued us for years start to disappear from our system. Maybe we become less judgemental of others or we don't compare ourselves so much. Whatever it is we have been struggling with may come down to us not really feeling at peace within. This is normal, and many people experience it. The practice of prayer and meditation are good practices to help with a greater sense of inner peace and offer an invitation to our inner self. In my experience, this inner self is the most valuable gift that we have as this is who we are.

Getting to know ourselves on such a deep level is both confounding and a joy. However, we experience this journey to the core of who we are it is not painless, but it is very rewarding. It takes time, effort and patience. But we are always aiming high and this can be one of our highest aims. To be rich in oneself and to be at ease with our inner qualities of love and creativity is beautiful.

Painting my pictures has made me happy along the way and the fact that I get to paint and create feels like a big part of my success story already. Writing for others helps me to share my ideas.

I bet that you have a success story embedded in your life's story as well. Whenever we have created something, made our life a little easier to live, or helped out someone else, we have paid some credit into our success account. We want to keep paying in this credit.

As artists, when we are being generous with ourselves and others we love and care about we are adding value to our lives and simultaneously elevating the perception of our profession, which is also important.

ART AS THE HEART'S LANGUAGE

Sometimes artists and art can seem undervalued, depending on many factors. But true art is always worthy! It ranks as high (to my mind) as all of the esteemed professions. Just keep in mind all the greats who have gone before us and made their contributions. Many were excellent men and women.

The language of art is a special language. Not everybody speaks it but almost everyone's heart can understand it. It bypasses the mind and goes straight to the heart. It is meant to make one feel. Of course, there is an intellectual approach to art as well and some people feel better or safer taking this approach, but if a work of art makes you feel something in your very essence, then it has the power to transform your world into something more colourful, beautiful and life enhancing. People who get into art get into a level of life that is rich, meaningful and enjoyable. They travel the world to see more beautiful paintings, visit cathedrals, gardens and fine places other people only dream about.

This is the joy and work of an artist. We exist to enhance the quality of people's lives, to touch their hearts and move their souls to creative expression. In the process we refine ourselves and are refined in turn. Once an artist – always an artist! From our very first tentative drawing to our next developing painting we are creating something special because it comes from within us. Art is one of the many professions where one gets to be their true self, and the creative expression it offers is a process of enjoyment. There is no art without the artist. And there is no artist without the human being who decides to be the best artist and person that he or she can be. This is our calling, our quest and our road to success.

FURTHER READING

The Lives of the Artists by Giorgio Vasari

Modern Man in Search of a Soul by Carl Jung

The Undiscovered Self by Carl Jung

Dreams by Carl Jung

Carl Jung: Wounded Healer of the Soul by Claire Dunne

Carl Jung and Soul Psychology by Donald Lathrop

The Artist's Way by Julia Cameron

The Agony and the Ecstasy by Irving Stone

The Highly Sensitive Person by Elaine Aron

The Language of Flowers by Vanessa Diffenbaugh

The Sunflower by Simon Wiesenthal

The Letters of Vincent Van Gogh by Vincent Van Gogh and Ronald de Leeuw

Do Protect, Legal Advice for Startups by Jonathan Rees

Angels 101 by Doreen Virtue

The Adventures of Huckleberry Finn by Mark Twain

Printed in January 2023
by Rotomail Italia S.p.A., Vignate (MI) - Italy